# THE BEAUTY OF THE MASS

## EXPLORING THE CENTRAL ACT OF CATHOLIC WORSHIP

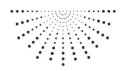

## CHARLES JOHNSTON

From Ante-Nicene Fathers, Vol. 5. Edited by Alexander Roberts, James Donaldson, and A. Cleveland Coxe. (Buffalo, NY: Christian Literature Publishing Co., 1886.) Revised and edited for New Advent by Kevin Knight.

Every reasonable effort has been made to determine copyright holders and secure permissions as needed. If any copyrighted material has been inadvertently used without proper credit being given in one manner or another, please notify publisher in writing so future editions may be corrected accordingly.

*To all Catholic Priests throughout the world,*

*Thank you for your dedication to God and His Church, and for offering the sacrifice of The Mass.*

*And especially to the priests of my parish,*

*Fr. Robert Seraph Aliunzi, A.J.*

*Fr. Teilo Lwande, A.J.*

*Fr. Edward Urassa, A.J.*

*Thank you for answering the call of the missionary, leaving your homes in Africa and coming to minister to your parishioners in the United States. We need holy priests like you, now more than ever.*

"If we really understood the Mass, we would die of joy."

Saint John Vianney

# INTRODUCTION

"My people are destroyed for lack of knowledge..."

— HOSEA 4:6

I have always been fascinated with liturgy and have been drawn to it since I was a child. While growing up I sometimes attended Mass with my mother and father (she is Catholic, he was Presbyterian), and sometimes the Sunday morning services at our local Presbyterian church (I'm not sure if all Presbyterian churches are liturgical, but the one we attended was), so any time I've visited a non liturgical church -most non-denominational and mega churches fit this category- I've felt out of place. They always felt like they were missing something, something I couldn't put my finger on.

As a teenager, and young adult, I attended non-denominational churches but always felt called back to liturgy. At first I thought this was only because of familiarity, being what I grew up with, but as I studied and read, it became clear to me that it wasn't just liturgy that was drawing me, but the ultimate pinnacle of the liturgy; the Holy Sacrifice of the Mass.

All liturgy has meaning, and in the Catholic Church this meaning builds until it reaches the pinnacle of all our worship; the re-presentation of Christ's sacrifice on Calvary! But even though the Eucharist is the pinnacle, and the consecration the path by which we climb to that summit, all the motions and words of the liturgy are filled with meaning. Every action of the priest, the deacon, the alter servers, and the parishioners has deep meaning and purpose, even if it may not be obvious to casual observers.

I am writing this because I've been asked many questions about the Mass over the years, both before I was Catholic -because I've always been "Catholic-ish"- and now much more since my conversion. I am not writing this because of any kind of special insight that I have into the deeper meanings of the Mass, I'm only hoping that I can point out some things you've maybe overlooked or have simply forgotten. I'm also not breaking any new theological grounds here, even though I've had many moments in Mass when a lightbulb seems to go off in my head, when I suddenly realized a formerly hidden connection between what I'm seeing and a passage from the Old Testament or the book of Revelation, only to discover that a Church Father had made that same connection 1600 years before me. There is nothing new under the sun, as King Solomon tells us, but if it's new to you then it's worth exploring and learning about.

This book has taken me over 2 years to write, but it also includes over a decade of studying liturgy, Catholic theology, and Sacred scripture. My conversion process was long and arduous, with many stops and starts, and in that time between Protestantism and Catholicism, I read anything and everything I could about the Mass. It's the fruits of this long process of research and study that I wish to share with my readers through this book.

## WHO I'M WRITING FOR

The people I'd like to reach through this book:

1. The cradle Catholic that has attended Mass for decades, and now maybe just goes through the motions without seeing the depth and beauty of

the Mass as it unfolds around them. You may
have learned everything that I write about years
ago, but over time you've forgotten, as it all just
became a Sunday routine. Any action performed
over a long period of time can become habitual
and lose its meaning, hopefully after reading this
you'll have a rekindled love for the Mass.

2. The cradle (or convert) Catholic that wasn't
   properly catechized and so has never heard the
   meanings behind the postures, words, and images
   of the Mass.

3. The Catholic that knows what I'm speaking of,
   the beauty and depth of the liturgy and will only
   nod along in agreement. Even though you might
   not learn anything new by reading this, I pray
   that you will be encouraged to continue seeing
   the beauty in our church.

4. The curious Protestant or non-believer who has
   an interest in the Mass but doesn't know why.
   You want to know what is happening, but don't
   know who to ask, or if you do ask you don't get
   satisfactory answers. Hopefully, I can try to
   provide some answers for your questions.

## LITURGY "ISN'T COOL"

Many contemporary Christians look down upon liturgy. They say church worship should be spontaneous and "spirit driven." To that I'd say two things. First, is that if God disapproved of liturgy and ritualistic worship, He sure had a strange way of showing it. The entire Old Testament economy of Salvation was based upon ritualistic worship and liturgical sacrifices, all laid out in precise details by God in the Torah. Secondly, "contemporary worship" is anything but spontaneous. It is ritual too, just less obviously so. Every Sunday the band spontaneously starts to play, and then the pastor just spontaneously decides to preach a prepared sermon, followed by a spontaneous altar call? No, it's all preplanned and laid out before the first person arrives.

The liturgy that we celebrate today is very similar in tone and character to the liturgy of the early Church. We can see this by reading the Church Fathers, especially Saint Justin Martyr's *First Apology,* but we can even see the liturgical structure in the pages of the New Testament. In Saint Luke's account of Jesus encountering His disciples on the road to Emmaus (Luke 24), we see several movements that are mirrored today; Jesus joins them on their journey, He breaks open the scriptures, and then He leads them in a Eucharistic "breaking of the bread." Following this pattern, the Church has always included both a

Liturgy of the Word and of the Eucharist in the Mass. These two parts "are so closely connected with each other that they form but one single act of worship." (*Sacrosanctum Concilium*, 56)

## THE LITURGY IS NOT EMPTY ROUTINE

If our approach to the movements, postures, and responses in the Mass is "I don't know, it's just what Catholics do" then we are not fully, actively, and consciously participating in the Mass like we're supposed to. To participate in the Mass to the fullest, and thus receive all the graces available through it, we must know what we are doing and why. This isn't an empty 2000, year old way to spend a Sunday morning, it's a public act of worship, established by the Church that Christ founded. It's one of, if not, the most important and fruitful things you can do with your time in this life.

---

"In the earthly liturgy we take part in a foretaste of that heavenly liturgy which is celebrated in the holy city of Jerusalem toward which we journey as pilgrims…"

— (*SACROSANCTUM CONCILIUM*, 8)

---

As I said before, what I want to point out in this book isn't anything new, but maybe it will be new to you. As a convert to the faith I sometimes see things differently than a cradle Catholic may see them because sometimes things look different from another perspective. I'd love for even just one person to come away from reading this book with a deeper understanding and love for our liturgy. A deeper sense that there is more happening than what appears on the surface, and there is even more happening beyond what we can see. If that were the only result of this entire project, then I'd say it was time well spent.

## THE MASS AS A SACRIFICE

Of all the many sacrifices and liturgies that have ever been offered to God, from Abraham's offerings in the deserts of the Levant; to the Tabernacle at Shilo; and the Temple in Jerusalem; to the present day, the liturgy of the Eucharist is the most sacred because it is a re-presentation (not a representation) of the ultimate sacrifice of Christ on Calvary. Because the debt incurred by mankind was infinite, only a sacrifice of infinite value would suffice to make satisfaction to the justice of God, Jesus paid the price as fully God and fully man. His life was of infinite value, and so His sacrifice was infinitely efficacious in the economy of our redemption.

Because the Mass is the same sacrifice of Calvary, made present to us today, the Catechism says that the Mass "completes and surpasses all the sacrifices of the Old Covenant" (*Catechism of The Catholic Church*, 1330).

It's the moment that we "join all the angels and saints" outside the limitations of time and space, and mystically be made present at the foot of the cross where Christ offers Himself as the sacrificial victim to ransom us from the bond of death.

To understand the Mass, you must understand the priesthood, and to understand the priesthood you must understand the Eucharist.

---

"The Eucharist is "the source and summit of the Christian life." "The other sacraments, and indeed all ecclesiastical ministries and works of the apostolate, are bound up with the Eucharist and are oriented toward it. For in the blessed Eucharist is contained the whole spiritual good of the Church, namely Christ himself, our Pasch."

— (CCC 1324)

---

Without Christ's real presence in the Blessed Sacrament,

the Mass is nothing more than just another "church service" among thousands of other denominations. But because of the sacrificial nature of the Mass, and its pinnacle in the Eucharist, we see it is a whole separate category from other Christians' church services. It's not a "service" in the sense used by other Christians because it's not being performed by men and directed towards God; it's being performed by a human priest, but he is acting on behalf of and in the person of Christ Himself, who is our High Priest and offered Himself to God the Father.

The sacrifice of the Mass is why we Catholics have priests and not "ministers." A priest is one who offers sacrifice, and only the Catholic Church (and our brethren to the east that have preserved Apostolic Churches) even claim to offer the sacrifice of Calvary. This is why our clergy are properly called priests, because they offer daily sacrifice to God, in an non-bloody manner, under the appearance of bread and wine.

If you understand what is happening before your eyes, you will understand that you are witnessing a miracle at every Mass you participate in.

---

"The sacrifice of Christ and the sacrifice of the Eucharist are one single sacrifice: "The victim is one and the same: the same now offers through the ministry of priests, who then offered himself on the cross; only the manner of offering is different." "And since in this divine sacrifice which is celebrated in the Mass, the same Christ who offered himself once in a bloody manner on the altar of the cross is contained and is offered in an un-bloody manner. . . this sacrifice is truly propitiatory."

— (CCC 1367)

---

The Catechism also teaches us that it is "Christ Himself," who acts "through the ministry of the priests, offers the Eucharistic sacrifice." It goes on to say that Jesus is the high priest and victim, that he offers Himself. (CCC 1410)

Without taking into account the sacrificial nature of the Mass, we can never fully grasp and understand what is taking place before our very eyes. The Mass becomes just another church service, and in a world where church services are loud and exciting, using fog machines and strobe lights, then the Mass is a comparatively boring service. But if we realize what is taking place, we can appreciate that the Mass is anything but just another "service."

I'm convinced that properly, and thoughtfully, cate-chizing lay Catholics on the nature of the Mass would make a major impact on keeping bodies in the pews and helping souls to heaven by remaining in the Church founded by Christ.

It's with this in mind, that the Second Vatican Council declared that we should have "full, active, and conscious participation" in the Mass.

---

"At the Last Supper, on the night when He was betrayed, our Saviour instituted the eucharistic sacrifice of His Body and Blood. He did this in order to perpetuate the sacrifice of the Cross throughout the centuries until He should come again, and so to entrust to His beloved spouse, the Church, a memorial of His death and resurrection: a sacrament of love, a sign of unity, a bond of charity, a paschal banquet in which Christ is eaten, the mind is filled with grace, and a pledge of future glory is given to us.

The Church, therefore, earnestly desires that Christ's faithful, when present at this mystery of faith, should not be there as strangers or silent spectators; on the contrary, through a good understanding of the rites and prayers they should take part in the sacred action, conscious of what they are doing, with devotion and full collaboration. They should be instructed by God's word and be nourished at the table of the Lord's body; they should give thanks to God by offering the Immaculate Victim, not only through the hands of the priest, but also with him, they should learn also to offer themselves; through Christ the Mediator, they should be drawn day by day into ever more perfect union with God and with each other, so that finally God may be all in all.

— (*SACROSANCTUM CONCILIUM,* 47 & 48)

---

So, let's dive deep into this sacred moment that we have the joy of witnessing every time we attend Mass.

(This book is written assuming the Ordinary Form of the Mass and in Ordinary Time. I'm not extremely familiar with the extraordinary form, and there are too many variables to account for in the different liturgical seasons... i.e. No Gloria in lent, or reading from Acts instead of the Old Testament during Easter season)

# THE INTRODUCTORY RITES

The Introductory Rites are a very brief portion of the Mass, but they are important because they help prepare us to part in the heavenly liturgy that is about to unfold before, and all around us. These Rites have a character of "beginning, introduction, and preparation," (*General Instructions of the Roman Missal*, 46) and so they hold an important place in our liturgical celebrations. They should be observed, and participated in, with all due reverence, and allow us to enter into a spirit of prayer and devotion.

---

"Their purpose is to ensure that the faithful who come together as one establish communion and dispose themselves to listen properly to God's word and to celebrate the Eucharist worthily."

— (*GIRM*, 46)

---

I've heard it said that Mass begins the moment you leave your house; it begins with a heart that desires to worship God. Our faith is one of action, we put our faith into motion and reach out to touch God's hand, as He stretches down to lift us up. We desire to be in a relationship with Him, and by doing so we enter into the spirit of the liturgy before the celebration even begins.

But before the actual start of Mass, be it leaving your house or the entrance procession, there are a few things that take place, things that aren't part of the Mass proper, but are part of the experience that is the Catholic Mass.

Sign of the Cross with Holy Water

Although not required by canon law, doctrine, dogma, precepts of the church, or dictates by the local ordinary (the bishop), almost everyone crosses themselves with holy water when entering the church.

The reasons why we bless ourselves with the sign of the cross are many, far too many to count, but I'll just say the most important one to me; it tells us by what price we were purchased. The price that Christ paid for us was an instrument of Roman torture, so painful that it is where we get the word "excruciating" from. That's how much God loves us, that He would take on flesh and sacrifice himself in the most humiliatingly painful way ever conceived in the minds of men. This was the price with which we were purchased, ransomed from sin and death, to be new creations in Christ.

The cross is our salvation and our hope, this is why we bless ourselves with what the secular world would see as a sign of shame. This is why Saint Paul said it's "foolishness" to those who don't believe. (1 Corinthians 1:23)

We use the holy water to make this sign of the Cross for a couple reasons; one is that holy water is a sacramental, and when used in a proper disposition, can confer upon a person actual graces from God. The other reason is to remind ourselves of our baptism, and the promises made, either by us or our parents on our behalf. In reminding ourselves of our baptism we renounce Satan, his works, his empty promises, and reaffirm our belief in God. We also are to resolve ourselves to live out these baptismal promises in our day to day lives.

## GENUFLECTION

This literally means to "bend the knee," in Latin. We genuflect towards the tabernacle because we believe that Christ is physically present in the Holy Eucharist that is contained in the tabernacle. We bend our knee in reverence for the Real Presence, the fact that the King of the Universe made Himself present to us in a physical way. We show reverence and respect for humans in everyday life, and special honor is reserved for heads of state, so how much more honor and respect should we show to the One who created all.

Most of the time the tabernacle is behind the main altar, but sometimes it is off to one side or the other. Look for the red lamp that is always lit in front of the tabernacle to find it more easily when visiting a new church. This lamp has come along to our faith from our Old Testament roots, God commanded Moses to keep a lamp eternally burning, the *ner tamid* was kept burning inside the Holy Place, by the Ark of the Covenant (Exodus 27:20-21). What is very interesting is that we know the ark contained three objects that foreshadowed Christ; the manna, the law, and Aaron's staff, and now we see the light shining just outside the ark, and Jesus is the light of the world. (John 8:12 & 9:5)

## THE MASS BEGINS

### THE ENTRANCE PROCESSION

One of the first things that immediately struck me as different about the Mass, in style not substance of course, was the entrance procession. The Presbyterian church I attended as a child had one, but every Protestant church I'd been to since then didn't, it's just not how "contemporary" Christians, of the Protestant variety, worship God. They are really missing out.

I once asked why there was a procession, and why the priest didn't just start the Mass up at the altar. The answer I received was a variation of "why do baseball players have 'walking up to bat' music?" If that doesn't sound right to you, it's because it isn't. The priest doesn't just choose a snappy tune and then dance down the main aisle. Like I said before; everything in the Mass has meaning and purpose, even just the way the priest enters the sanctuary.

The priest and ministers (deacon, altar server, and lectors) begin either just inside or just outside the rear door of the church. We stand at attention as a sign of respect for the priest, who during the liturgy will be representing Christ Himself, and for the book of the gospels that is usually carried aloft by the deacon. The procession is usually led by altar servers carrying candles that represent the Light of the World (Christ) and a crucifix is also carried.

So, if you looked at it another way; Christ (represented by the priest) processes through the Body of Christ (the assembled church members) while a deacon carries the Book of the Gospel (the actual words of Christ. And Christ being the Word made flesh) while altar servers carry the light of Christ (the candles), and another altar server carries an image of the crucified Christ. All this symbolism is profound, and the Mass has just started.

The procession ends at the altar where all bow, and after climbing the steps, both the priest and deacon kiss the altar as a sign of respect for the sacred sacrifice that will be presented there.

## THE SIGN OF THE CROSS

After the procession, the priest and deacon go to the presider's chair. When the music ends he makes The Sign of The Cross on himself, and the people do also.

The reason he does this is because the entire Mass is a prayer, and as Catholics we usually begin prayers by reminding ourselves of whose Name we are praying in, and by what price we can dare to approach God and pray, because only by the cross are we reconciled with God and able to so freely approach Him in prayer.

Afterwards he greets the people by saying a variation of "the Lord be with you," this is an ancient greeting found throughout the Old Testament, and we respond with, "and with your spirit."

## PENITENTIAL RITES

The priest invites us to call to mind our sins and ask for God's pardon, so as to prepare ourselves to take part in the Holy Sacrifice of the Mass. Just as we take part in the Introductory Rites to prepare our minds to enter the liturgy, we have to prepare our souls as well. The GIRM says that the Penitential Rites "lacks the efficacy of the Sacrament of Penance." (GIRM, 51) This means that the Penitential Rites are not a substitute for Sacramental Reconciliation and is only efficacious in the absolution of venial sins. If you are conscious of mortal sin, you are not reconciled to God through this Rite, and you should abstain from receiving the Eucharist until you receive absolution.

At this point the priest has a little leeway in how he chooses to proceed. He can either lead the people in the recitation of the Confiteor (I confess to almighty God...) or he can go straight to the Kyrie eleison (Lord have mercy). Whatever one he chooses is followed by him granting absolution (for venial sins) to the people.

The Confiteor is a beautiful prayer that acknowledges our sinfulness before God, and before our fellow parishioners. We are all sinners, and even the priest takes part in this prayer, because he too is human, and subject to the trials and temptations that we all endure. The Church is a hospital for sinners, and it's one of our greatest strengths that we recognize our sinfulness and brokenness at almost every Mass. As G.K. Chesterton so succinctly put it, "The great strength of Christian sanctity has always been simply this – that the worst enemies of the saints could not say of the saints anything worse than [the saints] said of themselves … Suppose the village atheist had a sudden and splendid impulse to rush into the village church and denounce everybody there as miserable offenders. He might break in at the exact moment when they were saying the same thing themselves."


## KYRIE ELEISON

After the Penitential Rite, the priest or deacon leads the people in singing or chanting the Kyrie Eleison (Greek: Lord have mercy). This is always said during Mass, but if used as the Penitential Rite instead of the Confiteor then it is not repeated.

Error

8

Kyrie Eleison is Greek, and some scholars point to the fact that this is one of the few remaining instances of Greek in the Roman liturgy, this being evidenced that the Kyrie Eleison predates the change in the western Church from Greek to Latin in the liturgy (5th or 6th century).

Even though this can sometimes be seen as groveling for mercy from a wrathful God, it really should be seen as prayer of praise for the mercy that God has shown us despite our unworthiness. This can be seen in the verses between the response, for example, "You were sent to heal the contrite of heart," "You came to call sinners," and "You are seated at the right hand of the Father to intercede for us." All of these are praises and thanksgiving for God's unending mercy.

## THE GLORIA

The Kyrie Eleison leads to the singing of God's praises in the Gloria. The Gloria is an ancient hymn of praise for the Trinity and has roots in the western Church from the mid 4th century when St Hillary of Poitiers translated it from its original Greek.

This hymn gets its name from its first line in Latin, "Gloria in excelsis Deo..." which is part of the greeting that an army of angels gave to the shepherds on that cold December night 2000 years ago, "And suddenly there was with the angel a multitude of the heavenly host praising God and saying, "Glory to God in the highest, and on earth peace among men with whom he is pleased!" (Luke 2:13-14. See also *The Catechism of The Catholic Church, 333*)

It is awe inspiring, whenever we are singing the Gloria, we are joining in with all the angels in heaven in their hymn of praise that continues for all time.

One of my most memorable times in Mass involved the Gloria. It was during the Easter vigil, the night I was received into the church, when we started singing the Gloria, the veil that was covering the crucifix behind the altar was dropped. I'm not an emotional person, I can count the times I've cried as an adult, and this was one of those times. The image of Christ being unveiled, just as we were singing that ancient hymn of praise (that we hadn't heard for the entire forty days of Lent), struck me as the most glorious, prayerful, spiritual and beautiful moment of worship that I'd ever been involved in.

There is more going on in the Mass than what you can see with your eyes. We believe that angels and devils are real; that there is more in this world than can be experienced with our limited ability to feel it; and there is an infinite metaphysical reality that just cannot be sensed with our finite senses. It is in this reality beyond our senses that the hymn of angelic Gloria never ends.

"Then I looked, and I heard around the throne and the living creatures and the elders, the voice of many angels, numbering myriads of myriads and thousands of thousands, saying with a loud voice, "Worthy is the Lamb who was slain, to receive power and wealth and wisdom and might and honor and glory and blessing!" And I heard every creature in heaven and on earth and under the earth and in the sea, and all therein, saying, "To him who sits upon the throne and to the Lamb be blessing and honor and glory and might for ever and ever!"

— (REVELATION 5:11-13)

So, the next time you don't feel like singing along, or are distracted by someone else's bad singing, or worry about your own, think of this scene from the Book of Revelation, and the "myriads of myriads" of angels and Saints praising God with you. And sing with all your heart!

THE COLLECT

After the Gloria, while we all remain standing, the priest once again calls the people to pray. This prayer is known as the Collect, because it collects all the prayers of the people as individuals and unites us as a community in prayer.

The Collect is sometimes called the "Opening prayer," but this is a misnomer because it actually closes out, rather than opens, the Introductory Rites of the Mass. The Collect, just like all the Introductory Rites, ensures that we, the Body of Christ, come together as one to praise, worship, and receive the Lord in a worthy and prayerful manner.

## END OF INTRODUCTORY RITES

When is one late?

There's a constant debate among Catholics of when someone is actually late for Mass. Opinions range from the consecration of the Host, to the praying of the Collect. With something of a consensus of opinions settling on the Collect as the point at which one is late, but since we've spent this time on how significant and theologically rich the Introductory Rites are, I'd say that they are more important than something that can easily be missed and still fulfill our Sunday obligation.

Priests constantly try to say Mass and have people on their way in a reasonable amount of time, and still if Mass goes beyond 60-70 minutes there is likely to be a riot in the parking lot (this says a lot about us -me included- that we can sit through a 4 hour long football game or 2 hour movie, but God forbid, that Father goes a little long in his homily). If the Introductory Rites were so inconsequential, no more important than the opening credits of a film, wouldn't the Church just remove them from the Order of the Mass and cut 10-15 minutes from the Mass? Since they haven't done so, it would seem to be good evidence of their importance in preparation for our celebration of these sacred mysteries.

So, come early, sing along during the procession, search your conscience during the Penitential Rite, remember the mercy of God durning the Kyrie Eleison, praise the glory of God during the Gloria, and allow your personal prayers to be gathered in and made one with all the prayers of the people during the Collect.

# 2

# LITURGY OF THE WORD

The structure of our liturgy today, follows that of the first Mass after the Resurrection; on the road to Emmaus. When Jesus met His disciples on the road, and was "hidden from their eyes," He first broke open the scriptures with them, before He broke bread and nourished them with the Eucharist. In today's Mass, we are nourished by the Word of God, both in the form of the scriptures being proclaimed, and in the Eucharistic meal.

The Catechism calls the liturgy the Word and the Eucharist "one single act of worship" (CCC 1346) and the same paragraph mentions how in our tradition, we are fed at the "Eucharistic table", by both "the Word of God and the Body of the Lord."

The Eucharist is described as the "source and summit

of the Christian faith," by so many Church documents, Church Fathers, and Popes. Then if you were to envision the Eucharist as the peak of a high mountain, the Liturgy of The Word can be thought of as the bedrock of that mountain, and also keeping with the mountain metaphor, it is the road that winds it's way to the peak while traveling through over 4000 years of Salvation History. To see see the importance the Church places on its foundation in scripture, read the Vatican II documents *Dei Verbum* and *Sacrosanctum Concilium.*

"Sacred scripture is of the greatest importance in the celebration of the liturgy. For it is from scripture that lessons are read and explained in the homily, and psalms are sung; the prayers, collects, and liturgical songs are scriptural in their inspiration and their force, and it is from the scriptures that actions and signs derive their meaning"

— (*SACROSANCTUM CONCILIUM*, 24)

It's the Scriptures that give the Eucharist its foundation, it's the backbone of our liturgical tradition. It's the

Liturgy of The Word that is the foundation of the next part of the Mass, the Liturgy of The Eucharist.

FIRST READING

The First Reading usually comes from the Old Testament, that being the part of the Bible written before the incarnation of Christ, sometimes called the Hebrew Bible. These scriptures are considered the Word of God by both Christians and Jews.

Even though some people may consider the Old Testament "out of date" or even "canceled out by the New Testament," this is actually a heresy that is called Marcionism. Named after its founder, Marcion of Sinope, this heresy was condemned by many of the early Church Fathers. Ironically, Marcionism held to a Biblical canon that included only the Gospel of Luke and the Pauline Epistles, but it was St. Paul himself that tells us of the value of the Old Testament. In his letter to the Romans he wrote,

"For whatever was written in former days was written for our instruction, that by steadfastness and by the encouragement of the Scriptures we might have hope."

The scriptures that Saint Paul was referring to, were the writings of the Old Testament, they are still valid, they still contain the inspired Word of God, and they are still there to offer us encouragement and hope.

They also provide much needed context to understand the Gospel as Jews of the time of Christ would have. We proclaim in the Creed, every Sunday, that we believe Christ rose from the dead "in accordance with the Scriptures," but what scriptures? How can we know what we proclaim without examining these scriptures ourselves? This is why the Old Testament remains indispensable to the life of the Church and to all Christians. We should be well versed in the history and story of salvation, so as to know the foundations of our beliefs, and the very foundation of the Church. The New Testament is not "more important" or "more inspired" than the Old, they both are equally breathed into existence by the Holy Spirit and are both for our benefit.

The Old Testament readings do not follow a pattern through each book but are placed in the lectionary (the book of readings that we use in Mass) to compliment and supplement the Gospel reading. The themes in the First Reading will be echoed in the Gospel that Sunday, this is why, when personally preparing for Sunday's liturgy, I like to read the Gospel Reading first and then the First Reading, followed by the Second Reading.

## RESPONSORIAL PSALM

After the First Reading comes the Responsorial Psalm. This extension of the Old Testament reading is part scripture reading, part sacred music (because preferentially the Responsorial Psalm is to always be sung), and part prayer.

Praying with the Psalms is an ancient practice in the Church that goes all the way back to our Jewish roots. Today in our Catholic tradition you will find priests, religious, and the laity all around the world praying the liturgy of the hours, which is composed primarily from the Book of Psalms. If you were to travel to Israel, and visit the Western Wall, you'd find Jews praying these same Psalms, just as Jesus would've in His day.

---

"The Psalms both nourished and expressed the prayer of the People of God gathered during the great feasts at Jerusalem and each Sabbath in the synagogues. Their prayer is inseparably personal and communal; it concerns both those who are praying and all men. The Psalms arose from the communities of the Holy Land and the Diaspora, but embrace all creation. Their prayer recalls the saving events of the past, yet extends into the future, even to the end of history; it commemorates the promises God has already kept, and awaits the Messiah who will fulfill them definitively. Prayed by Christ and fulfilled in him, the Psalms remain essential to the prayer of the Church."

— (CCC 2586)

Praying with the Psalms is, and was, such a common practice among the Jews that one of the last things Jesus said on the cross was a quote from the Psalms.

"And about the ninth hour Jesus cried with a loud voice, " Eli, Eli, la'ma sabach'-tha'ni?" that is, "My God, my God, why have you forsaken me?"

— (MATTHEW 27:46)

Jesus was quoting the first verse of Psalm 22, and contrary to popular opinion, Jesus wasn't giving into despair or admitting that the Father had abandoned Him, He was praying a Psalm that begins with despair but ends with a hope for deliverance by God. Jesus was very intimately connected to the Psalms, and so should we be, because they can teach us how to better pray.

## PRAY LIKE KING DAVID

The majority of the Psalms were written by king David, an ancestor of Jesus, and a foreshadowing or type of Christ. King David was described as a "man after God's own heart" (1 Sam 13:14) and since he wrote the Psalms as cries from the heart, with the inspiration of the Holy Spirit, the Church teaches us that the Psalms can help us to pray like King David prayed.

> "David is par excellence the king "after God's own heart," the shepherd who prays for his people and prays in their name. His submission to the will of God, his praise, and his repentance, will be a model for the prayer of the people. His prayer, the prayer of God's Anointed, is a faithful adherence to the divine promise and expresses a loving and joyful trust in God, the only King and Lord. In the Psalms David, inspired by the Holy Spirit, is the first prophet of Jewish and Christian prayer. The

prayer of Christ, the true Messiah and Son of David, will reveal and fulfill the meaning of this prayer."

— (CCC 2579)

---

## THE SECOND READING

This reading is always from the New Testament, unlike the First Reading and the Psalm that was sung.

The importance of these Books and Letters of the New Testament cannot be overstated. While the Words of Christ, and His teachings are found in the Gospels, the other New Testament books, written by men like Saints Paul, Peter, James, and John expand on and explain some of the teachings and actions of Christ.

The Second Reading runs through each book, one at a time, and is untethered to the Gospel reading, unlike the First Reading which is chosen for the lectionary to complement the Gospel reading. If you look at the Sunday readings, you will notice that each Sunday the Second Reading progresses through Romans, 1 Corinthians, Ephesians, and so on. While the First Readings will skip between Exodus one week and Ezekiel the next, depending on that week's Gospel reading.

The Second Reading takes in the pastoral advice of these Apostles, and it absorbs them in toto, as a whole letter and not broken up each week, just as we read an entire Gospel at a time. These New Testament Epistles are actually a great place to start if someone wants to begin a serious study of Sacred Scripture, because they explain the Gospel and Doctrines of the Church in a very pastoral and understandable way.

## THE GOSPEL

The Gospel reading is the pinnacle of the Liturgy of The Word. It is in the Gospel that we hear proclaimed the very words and deeds of Christ. The Gospel reading, and it's accompanying symbolism, is so rich that it will need a thorough examination.

The GIRM says that the Gospel is "the high point of the Liturgy of the Word," and that "the Liturgy itself teaches that great reverence" is to be shown to it by setting it apart from the other readings with extra pomp and ceremony (*GIRM*, 60)

Also, during the proclamation of the Gospel we will come across the first of many quiet prayers and actions of the Priest and/or Deacon that largely goes unnoticed by the faithful. Even if they are noticed, they go unheard because the rubrics of the Mass indicates they are to be said "in a low voice."

(These "secret prayers," as they are sometimes called, are not actually a secret because they're available for all to read in the GIRM and the Roman Missal, but they are unknown to many of the faithful, so they are akin to a secret. The Church isn't hiding anything from us, but in her wisdom, she chose to have these prayers said low for reasons unknown to me, but they point to some great symbolism and theology, so I'd like to share them in this examination of the Liturgy.)

## LITURGICAL CYCLES

You may have noticed that the Gospel readings stay in one book of the Gospels throughout a given year (with some exceptions), this is due to what we call Liturgical Cycles.

Cycles A, B, and C go through the Gospels of Matthew, Mark, and Luke. The Gospel of John is read around Christmas, during Lent, and during the Easter season through all three cycles.

Although there are twenty-seven books in the New Testament, there are only four Gospels, so every Mass, 364 days a year (there is no Mass on Good Friday, the only day of the year that there isn't), you will hear a reading proclaimed from one of these four.

## ALL RISE

Just as we rise for the Priest during the entrance procession, we also stand during the reading of the Gospel. The reason is respect and reverence, the Gospels contain the words of Christ, and His words deserve the utmost respect, we show this respect and honor by rising, the same way as gentlemen did in years past when a lady entered the room, or when the judge enters the courtroom. Our posture in Mass also indicates what we are doing in that moment; sitting to learn from the readings and homily; standing for the procession and prayer; and kneeling in reverence for Christ made present on the altar.

Rising for the Gospel also has biblical precedent. When the priest Ezra read from the Scriptures, all the people rose in a showing of reverence towards the Law and God.

"And Ezra opened the book in the sight of all the people, for he was above all the people; and when he opened it all the people stood."

— (NEHEMIAH 8:6)

## THE ALLELUIA

The cantor, or choir, leads the people in the singing of the Alleluia. Alleluia, also translated as hallelujah, comes from a Hebrew expression that means "praise the Lord." It is believed to have been chanted by the Levitical Priests during Temple liturgies in Jerusalem.

Found throughout the psalms, notably in Psalm 150 and in Tobit's prayer of praise, in which he describes the New Jerusalem with the words "hallelujah."

> "The streets of Jerusalem will be paved with beryl and ruby and stones of O'phir; all her lanes will cry 'Hallelujah!' and will give praise, saying, 'Blessed is God, who has exalted you for ever.'"
>
> — (TOBIT 13:18)

Interestingly, the only time hallelujah appears in the New Testament is in Saint John's vision of heavenly praises. These praises are mirrored, and joined by us in the Mass.

"After this I heard what seemed to be the mighty voice of a great multitude in heaven, crying, "Hallelujah! Salvation and glory and power belong to our God." And the twenty-four elders and the four living creatures fell down and worshiped God who is seated on the throne, saying, "Amen. Hallelujah!" And from the throne came a voice crying, "Praise our God, all you his servants, you who fear him, small and great." Then I heard what seemed to be the voice of a great multitude, like the sound of many waters and like the sound of mighty thunderpeals, crying, "Hallelujah! For the Lord our God the Almighty reigns."

— (REVELATION 19:1,4-6)

We can see that hallelujah was proclaimed by King David in the psalms, chanted by the priests in God's temple, envisioned to be sung by the "great multitude" in Saint John's vision of heaven, and according to Tobit it could be considered the anthem of the New Jerusalem (also heaven).

Is it any wonder that we joyfully sing the Alleluia before reading the very words of The Word made flesh? The turning point of history, the moment that divides time, when God came down from heaven and clothed Himself in human flesh, all for the redemption of mankind. Really, we should sing alleluia just thinking about it, and not only in Mass, but even when walking down the street!

## THE PRIEST'S BLESSING

As the people sing the alleluia, the Deacon rises and bows his head before the presiding Priest and asks for his blessing.

The Priest quietly prays over him,

---

May the Lord be in your heart and on your lips, that you may proclaim his Gospel worthily and well, in the name of the Father and of the Son and of the Holy Spirit."

---

If there is no Deacon present during the Mass, the priest will proclaim the Gospel himself, and before doing so he bows at the altar and says,

---

"Cleanse my heart and my lips, almighty God, that I may worthily proclaim your holy Gospel."

## CANDLES

This one is a hit or miss, you may or may not see this at your local parish depending on availability of altar servers, a deacon, and the preference of the pastor, but I will mention it here because of its beautiful symbolism.

According to the rubrics (GIRM 117), the altar must have at least two candles on it, or beside it, during Mass. That is a must, but processing with the candles and moving them to the ambo is optional.

Just as everyone rises, the altar servers will remove two candles from the altar and place them by the ambo (the stand at which the readings are proclaimed). These candles serve the purpose of symbolizing the light of Christ that enters in the procession, are placed on the altar, and then moved to the ambo, where the light of Christ will shine forth through His very words. They are then moved back to the altar to be a witness to the sacrifice of Calvary that is made present on the altar.

## SIGN BEFORE THE GOSPEL

After greeting the people, the Deacon, or Priest, says:

"A reading from the Gospel according to N."

---

At these words he makes the sign of the cross on his forehead, lips, and chest. This is a prayer through movement, much as the sign of the cross is itself a silent prayer, or genuflecting before the tabernacle.

We mimic this movement, and in doing so we are praying that God's word be always on our mind, on our lips, and residing in our hearts. This is a prayer that we, as Catholics, should be praying daily, even hourly. We need Christ on our minds throughout the day, we need the good news to be on our lips at all times, and we need the love of God to always reside in our hearts and lead us to follow His will.

## AFTER THE GOSPEL

After the usual response from the people, the Deacon or Priest, kisses the book of the Gospels and says quietly,

---

"Through the words of the Gospel may our sins be wiped away."

---

This is another prayer that should be in our hearts at all

times. That by reading and meditating on the Word of God we may be conformed to be more like Him. This is the very essence of praying with the scriptures, that through meditating on the Word of God we may be changed and made to more closely follow His will.

## THE HOMILY

I've heard it said that the homily is not a very important part of the Mass, its "just Father's opinion. Everybody has an opinion, so why does his matter so much?" But this sentiment couldn't be more wrong.

First, our priests are called father because they are the spiritual fathers of the parishes that are our spiritual families, I'd hate for my children to disrespect what I had to say and brush it aside so easily. That being said, priests are not infallible, so if he says something that sounds off, or maybe espouses an opinion that is heterodox, approach him afterwards and discuss it, but whatever you do don't just start talking about him behind his back.

Second, the homily is a very important part of the Mass that is mentioned in both the *GIRM* (paragraph 65) and *Sacrosanctum Concilium(52)*. One reason why the homily is important, so important that it can't be omitted except for a "serious reason," can be found in Luke 24. In the story about the road to Emmaus, Jesus recounts several scriptures and then explains the meaning of many prophecies concerning Himself to His disciples before having a Eucharistic meal with them. If this structure sounds familiar, it's because it is, and we see it at every Mass we attend. I thought it was just me, the first time I read the story of Emmaus after becoming Catholic, I thought I'd had an epiphany, but then I read the catechism and saw it right there,

---

"Is this not the same movement as the Paschal meal of the risen Jesus with his disciples? Walking with them he explained the Scriptures to them; sitting with them at table "he took a bread, blessed and broke it, and gave it to them."

— (CCC 1347)

---

The Ethiopian eunuch asked Saint Philip how was he supposed to understand the scriptures "unless someone taught him."(Acts 8:31) The Ethiopian eunuch realized something that has passed over the head of far too many people, that without the guiding influence of the Church and it's magisterial teaching authority, people come to vastly different conclusions based on scriptures taken out of context. We must read, and listen to, the scriptures within this contextual framework, and so the homily remains an important part of the liturgy.

After the homily a brief moment of silence is "appropriately observed."

If you're like me you probably thought Father just took a micro nap in his chair, or was lost in thought, but this silence is actually prescribed in the rubrics of the Mass. It's a moment for all of us to meditate and reflect on the Gospel reading and how it was presented to us in the homily, along with any challenges issued by the homilist to better live our Christian lives.

## THE CREED

All rise again to profess our faith. Usually in the form of the Nicene Creed, although the Apostles' Creed may also be used, especially in Masses for children. We profess our beliefs as a body, but as an individual profession of faith. The *GIRM* points out that we profess our belief in the sacred mysteries of the Church, just before "these mysteries are celebrated in the Eucharist." (*GIRM*, 67)

The Creed is a subject worthy of its own book, or even a series of books, and there have been many great books written on just this one portion of the Mass. I'd only like to point out something that I find remarkable; we profess our belief in God the Father, The Son, and The Holy

Spirit, and in doing so we profess belief in the natures of these three Persons of the Holy Trinity.

By far, the longest section is the part about who Jesus is, and what He has done. But there isn't even one mention of His teachings. This isn't because the Church, or even the Father's of the First councils of Nicaea and Constantinople (where the Nicene Creed was debated and promulgated), were unconcerned with the teachings of Christ, it's because by having a correctly formed belief in the "ousia" or being of Christ helps us to better understand and have correct opinions on the teachings of Christ. That's because His teachings flow from His being, and to know one helps demystify the other.

We also affirm our faith in the Four Marks of the Church. We say that we believe the Church is One, Holy, Catholic, and Apostolic. These marks are very important to the Nature day mission of the Church and are necessary to discern what Church (out of all the possible claimants) is the one, true Church, founded by Christ on His apostles. (See Appendix B for a detailed exposition on the Four Marks of the Church)

## THE PRAYERS OF THE FAITHFUL

We remain standing while the Priest or Deacon read off a series of prayer intentions to which we make the usual response, "Lord, hear our prayer."

This is a time for us to join in the prayers of our parish, our diocese, our nation, and the universal Church. This is not a time to mindlessly drone back the response without any prayer or meaning behind it, we are to pray along, not just repeat the words. These prayers often end with opportunity to silently make our own petitions to God.

# 3

# LITURGY OF THE EUCHARIST

## THE OFFERTORY

After the prayers of the faithful, the gifts are brought to the altar. These gifts are the bread and wine, the elements that will be offered to God as a sacrifice and will miraculously become the Body, Blood, Soul, and Divinity of our Lord and Savior Jesus Christ.

In days gone by, the faithful baked the bread and made the wine that was used by the priest during the Mass, but today the hosts are purchased from special manufacturers and the wine is often bought in a supermarket. The faithful still brings these gifts to the altar to represent the "gifts" that each Catholic brings to the Church, and gives it willingly as their time, talent, and treasure, to be used to build up the Kingdom here on earth. It also represents our participation in the sacrifice that will take place, as the priest later says, "that my sacrifice and yours..."

The use of bread and wine actually has deeper meaning, other than the obvious one of it being what Jesus consecrated at the Last Supper. Bread and wine, especially in the context of a covenant meal, has very deep roots in the Old Testament. The very first person to be called a priest in the Bible, Melchizedek, the King of Salem, brought out bread and wine when he blessed Abraham.

"And Melchizedek king of Salem brought out bread and wine; he was priest of God Most High."

— (GENESIS 14:18)

Melchizedek is a type, or foreshadowing, of Christ (with some people even taking the position that he was a pre-incarnation appearance of the Logos of God, The Second Person of the Holy Trinity). Also, when a priest is ordained, he is ordained into the priestly order of Melchizedek and not of the Aaronic priesthood (Hebrews 6:20). This sacrifice that is offered by the priest is a sacrifice of thanksgiving, just like the sacrifice of Melchizedek, because the word Eucharist means "thanksgiving" in Greek. The Catechism recognizes this prefigurement of the Eucharist in the sacrifice of Melchizedek,

---

"The Church sees in the gesture of the king-priest Melchizedek, who "brought out bread and wine," a prefiguring of her own offering."

— (CCC 1333)

---

## THE PREPARATION OF THE GIFTS

In the preparation of the Gifts, especially the prayer over the gifts, we see clearly that the Holy Sacrifice of the Mass is inextricably linked to the institution of the Eucharist at the Last Supper. Since the Last Supper was a Passover celebration, it only makes sense that many elements in the Liturgy of the Eucharist shares themes and symbols with the Jewish Passover.

Saint Paul likened our Eucharistic celebration with the feast of Passover, and the early fathers called the Passion and resurrection of Christ, and by extension the Eucharist, "the Passover of Christ."

---

"Cleanse out the old leaven that you may be new

dough, as you really are unleavened. For Christ, our Paschal Lamb, has been sacrificed. Let us, therefore, celebrate the festival, not with the old leaven, the leaven of malice and evil, but with the unleavened bread of sincerity and truth."

— (1 CORINTHIANS 5:7-8)

During the preparation of the gifts, and the instruments on the altar, such as the paten and corporal, you may notice the deacon, or the priest, pouring a small amount of water into the wine in the chalice.

The are several reasons for this mingling of water and wine, but the primary reason is because that's how Jesus would've prepared the cup that He gave to His disciples at the Last Supper. It was a common practice in the ancient world to dilute wine before serving it, but it was especially prescribed in the Passover liturgy that Christ and His disciples were celebrating on the night of the last supper.

The Haggadah (the book that lays out the liturgy of the Seder meal, or you could say it's the Jewish equivalent of the GIRM) prescribes the way the meal is to be eaten, and the dishes to be served, including the mingling of water and wine. The Babylonian Talmud even says exactly how much water to put into the wine.

This all took on deep messianic symbolism by the early Church Fathers; with some seeing it as a representation of the water and blood that flowed from Christ's side on the cross; others saw the wine as a representation of Christ, and the water as the Church, joined together in one cup; and still others looked at it as the hypostatic union of Christ's divinity and humanity.

I think it represents all of those aforementioned opinions, but when it is mixed, a prayer is prayed that gives light to how the Church sees it. Not that it invalidates the other symbols, but that it chose this one symbol to highlight in the liturgy. As the priest or deacon mixes the two, he prays these words quietly,

"By the mystery of this water and wine, may we come to share in the divinity of Christ, who humbled himself to share in our humanity."

These words are not usually heard by the faithful, unless the church is silent, and you are sitting very near to the altar, but they are exceedingly rich theologically. The fact that God became man to allow us to have a share in His divinity is one of the central mysteries of faith. We become "partakers of the Divine Nature" (2 Peter 1:4) of God every time we receive Him the the Most Holy Eucharist. (CCC 1129 & 1997)

(This next part of the liturgy, from this point until the priest says, "pray brethren...", may be said aloud for the congregation to hear, or may be said quietly while a song plays, and the offering is taken up. It's up to the discretion of the celebrant)

After the gifts are brought forward, the priest prays over them with these words. First taking the bread he prays,

> "Blessed are you, Lord God of all creation, for through your goodness we have received the bread we offer you: fruit of the earth and work of human hands, it will become for us the bread of life."

And the people respond with,

> "Blessed be God forever."

Then the priest takes the chalice and prays over it,

"Blessed are you, Lord God of all creation, for through your goodness we have received the wine we offer you: fruit of the vine and work of human hands, it will become our spiritual drink."

And once again we respond with,

"Blessed be God forever."

When Jesus and His disciples ate meals together, and when they celebrated the Last Supper, He would have said blessings over the bread and wine that would sound very similar to the prayers over the gifts that we hear at every Mass. Since Christianity comes from Jewish roots, this similarity shouldn't surprise us at all.

Here is the Jewish blessing of bread and wine to compare with the prayer over the gifts,

*"Blessed are You, Lord our God, King of the*

*Universe, who brings forth bread from the earth."*

*"Blessed are You, Lord our God, King of the*

*Universe, who creates the fruit of the vine."*

Almost the same words, because it carries the same meaning and purpose; to give thanks to the Creator, and King of the Universe, for everything we have and fir His very act of being.

After these prayers of blessings over the bread and wine, the priest bows and says in a low voice,

"With humble spirit and contrite heart may we be accepted by you, O Lord, and may our sacrifice in your sight this day be pleasing to you, Lord God."

This is another of the several quiet prayers that the faithful rarely hear. And like the last one, it is a very beautiful prayer that shows the servant's heart that the priest is supposed to have. A Catholic priest is not the high official, like pagan priests were in the ancient world, he is a servant of the people, and he reminds himself of this fact at every Mass. This is why one of the Pope's titles is "Servant of the Servants of God" because he has an important job to shepherd the people, but not to rule them as an absolute tyrant.

This prayer is also very similar to prayer that Azariah prayed while in the furnace in the Book of Daniel,

---

"Yet with a contrite heart and a humble spirit may we be accepted, as though it were with burnt offerings of rams and bulls, and with tens of thousands of fat lambs"

— (DANIEL 3:39)

---

## LAVABO

At this part of the Mass, the priest turns from the altar and washes his hands with the help of the altar servers or the deacon. This may come as a surprise to many, but this hand washing is actually the second time the priest washes his hands as part of the Mass; the first time takes place when he is vesting (putting on his liturgical clothing) in the sacristy and is part of a series of prayers called the vesting prayers.

While he washes his hands, he says this prayer that is taken from Psalms 51:2,

"Wash me, O Lord, from my iniquity and cleanse me from my sin."

This is a classic penitential psalm, asking God to renew the psalmist's heart and cleanse him from his sins.

Many Catholics will link this hand washing to the way Pilate washes his hands during Christ's Passion. But the priest is not acting "in persona Pilate" as it were, he is performing his priestly duties of offering sacrifice to God *In Persona Christi.*

In the letter to the Hebrews, it is revealed that Christ is our High Priest, and He is also the sacrificial victim who offers Himself on the altar for the atonement of the whole world.

"Since then we have a great high priest who has passed through the heavens, Jesus, the Son of God, let us hold fast our confession."

— (HEBREWS 14:4)

So, for the priest to wash his hands of the "guilt" of the

sacrifice doesn't make sense. But hand washing, as a liturgical act, actually predates the Passion of Our Lord by about 1300 years.

---

"The LORD said to Moses, "You shall also make a laver of bronze, with its base of bronze, for washing. And you shall put it between the tent of meeting and the altar, and you shall put water in it, with which Aaron and his sons shall wash their hands and their feet. When they go into the tent of meeting, or when they come near the altar to minister, to burn an offering by fire to the LORD, they shall wash with water, lest they die. They shall wash their hands and their feet, lest they die: it shall be a statute for ever to them, even to him and to his descendants throughout their generations."

— (EXODUS 30:17-21)

---

At the Council of Jerusalem, that is recorded in the Acts of the Apostles, the Apostles declared that we are no longer bound by the ceremonial Law of the Old Covenant, only the moral law remains obligatory to us. So then why did we keep this ceremonial act of washing, and why is it done so publicly beside the altar? Because the Church is reminding us, not with words, but with actions visible before us, that the Mass is a sacrifice, and the priest is preparing himself to offer that sacrifice!

Through this pray, in words and actions, we are reminded of the ancient formula *Lex Orandi, Lex Credendi* (Latin: "the law of praying is the law of believing). This motto of the early Church Fathers means that what, and how, we pray proclaims what we believe.

ORATE, FRATRES

Orate Fratres (Latin: "pray brethren"), at this command we stand at attention.

When we pray at Mass, there are two possible positions, one is standing, and the other kneeling. During the coming Eucharistic prayer, we will employ both positions. Kneeling in reverence and petition during the *Epiclesis* and *Anamnesis*, and standing as the body of Christ, the Church Militant, at the Lord's Prayer.

What is often overlooked is that the priest says, "my sacrifice and yours." What then is our sacrifice? Our sacrifice is the daily crosses that we carry, all our cares and our worries, all our sufferings, and all our intentions. (*Mediator Dei,* 91-93)

The Saints have said that if you could see with spiritual eyes, you'd see your guardian angel walking up to the altar and offering your intentions with those of the priest, uniting our sacrifice with that of the Mass.

Also, in this prayer, the priest is preparing to bring the offering of this sacrificial victim to the very throne of God. He is preparing for this miraculous moment by petitioning God to accept this sacrifice on behalf of His people and preparing for the moment when we enter into the timeless sacrifice of Calvary.

We pray that the Lord will accept the sacrifice at the hands of the priest, and we are "uniting ourselves to this entreaty"(*GIRM,* 77) that the the sacrifice is both ours and the priests and it is being accomplished for not just all present, but for the "the good of all His {God's} holy church."

## THE EUCHARISTIC PRAYER

The Eucharistic prayer itself has several variations; Eucharistic Prayer I (The Roman Canon), Eucharistic Prayer II, Eucharistic Prayer III, and Eucharistic Prayer IV, all having their own preface. But even with this wide variety of options presented to the presiding priest, there are commonalities between all the prayers. For this reason, we will focus less on the words of the

Eucharistic prayers themselves, and more on the common elements of the prayers. The Eucharist is described as "the source and summit of our faith," and the liturgy of the Eucharist as "the summit of the Mass," so then this Eucharistic Prayer is the center of the Mass.

The GIRM says that the Eucharistic prayer is the "center and summit of the entire celebration," and that "the meaning of the Prayer is that the entire congregation of the faithful should join itself with Christ in confessing the great deeds of God and in the offering of Sacrifice." It goes on to say that "The Eucharistic Prayer demands that all listen to it with reverence and in silence" because of its centrality to the liturgy, it is to be treated with the utmost reverence. (*GIRM*, 78)

This is the pinnacle that the rest of the liturgy has wound its way up to, it is the peak of this mountain, and aptly so, because it is on this mountain top, that we will mystically be at the foot of the cross of Christ, who was crucified on the mount of Calvary.

This is also the worship that Jesus described to the Samaritan woman in John 4, when He said that "an hour is coming when neither on this mountain nor in Jerusalem will you worship the Father." (John 4:21) Jesus envisioned His Church worshiping God in every place, and at every time, one earth. This is a fulfillment of the prophecy of Malachi, that a pure offering will be offered to the Lord from all nations,

---

"For from the rising of the sun to its setting my name is great among the nations, and in every place incense is offered to my name, and a pure offering; for my name is great among the nations, says the LORD of hosts."

— (MALACHI 1:11)

---

And these words are echoed before the Epiclesis in Eucharistic Prayer III,

---

"You are indeed Holy, O Lord, and all you have created rightly gives you praise, for through your Son our Lord Jesus Christ, by the power and working of the Holy Spirit, you give life to all things and make them holy, and you never cease to gather a people to yourself, so that from the rising of the sun to its setting a pure sacrifice may be offered to your name."

— (*ROMAN MISSAL,* EUCHARISTIC
PRAYER II)

## SURSUM CORDA

While not a part of the Eucharistic Prayer itself, it not being one of the eight constituent elements that the *GIRM* lays out in paragraph 79, the Sursum Corda (Latin: "lift up your hearts") is included in the portion of the Missal that includes the Eucharistic Prayer. It is really a greeting, dialogue, and urging by the priest to prepare ourselves for this portion of the Mass.

This is one of the most ancient parts of the entire Mass. The Mass is the same sacrifice of Calvary, and of the Last Supper, but it has changed in word and style over the years (the most obvious to us in this era would be the changes made during Vatican II), and yet it is the same, and retains some of its ancient prayers, this prayer is one of them. The earliest we can trace this introduction of the Eucharistic Prayer, is to Saint Hippolytus of Rome, a bishop and historian from the 2nd century. This prayer is included in all the liturgies of the Apostolic Churches (along with the Catholic Church, this includes the Eastern Orthodox and Oriental Orthodox Churches).

What does it mean to "lift up our hearts"? Many times, in the Old Testament it is said that we lift our souls and hearts to God in prayer. Several times in the Psalms, David says he lifts his soul to the Lord,

"To you, O LORD, I lift up my soul."

— (PSALMS 25:1)

"Gladden the soul of your servant, for to you, O Lord, do I lift up my soul."

— (PSALMS 86:4)

We "lift up our hearts" to God, and in doing so we enter into this mystery that is about to take place. We are about to be present at the recapitulation of the sacrifice of Calvary, a bloody sacrifice that is re-presented in an unbloody manor, in the same way that Last Supper was the same sacrificial action of Calvary, and the fulfillment of The Passover, but done in an un-bloody manor. Just as St John was told to "come up here," we are about to enter into the worship of God that is described in Revelation (see also CCC 1090),

"After this I looked, and behold, in heaven an open door! And the first voice, which I had heard speaking to me like a trumpet, said, "Come up here, and I will show you what must take place after this." At once I was in the Spirit, and behold, a throne stood in heaven, with one seated on the throne!"

— (REVELATION 4:1-3)

---

This phrase also means to set our mind and heart on the things of God, to focus on Him, and to worship Him. We are entering into this most mystical and important phase of the liturgy, and we must lift our hearts and entire beings up from the cares of this world, and we must place them at the feet of God in Heaven. We have to lift up our hearts to God, elevate the desires of our hearts, and remain in that elevated state throughout the rest of the Mass.

Saint Cyprian of Carthage, writing around AD 250, describes the meaning of this prayer,

---

"Moreover, when we stand praying, beloved brethren, we ought to be watchful and earnest with our whole heart, intent on our prayers. Let all carnal and worldly thoughts pass away, nor let the soul at that time think on anything but the object only of its prayers. For this reason, also the priest, by way of preface before his prayers, prepares the minds of the brethren by saying, "Lift up your hearts," that so upon the people's response, "We lift them up unto the Lord," he may be reminded that he himself ought to think of nothing but the Lord. Let the breast be closed against the adversary, and be open to God alone..."

— (*TREATISE 4*, P31)

He goes on to describe the Devil trying to distract us during prayer, and how this prayer is a reminder to lift our hearts to Lord and to focus our attention on the miracle that is about to happen.

## THE ANAPHORA

The Eucharist Prayer, also known as the Anaphora, has eight distinct elements. These elements are described in *GIRM*, paragraph 79. We will look at the list, and then go deeper into each element:

1. Thanksgiving. This is expressed mainly throughout the preface.
2. Acclimation. In which we join with all those in heaven to sing praises to our God.
3. Epiclesis. Here the priest prays for Holy Spirit to descend upon the gifts on the altar.
4. Institution narrative and consecration. Through the actual words of Christ, and by the priest's hands, the Bread and wine become the Body and blood of Jesus.
5. Anamnesis. This element revolves around memory. We remember what Christ has done for us, as we keep His command to "do this in memory of me."
6. Offering. This sacrifice, of His Son, is offered to God the Father.
7. Intersessions. We are reminded here, that this sacrifice is not just for those present, or even just for the Church of the living, but it is being offered for all people and in all times.
8. Final Doxology. A short prayer of praise that also serves to remind us that everything, and every part of the Church revolves around Christ.

These are the elements that make up this one prayer, now we can focus on each one individually.

## THE PREFACE

The preface to the Eucharistic Prayer is filled with thanksgiving, because it is "our duty and salvation, always and everywhere to give you {God} thanks." When we reply, "it is right and just" to the priest's invitation to give thanks to God, we are saying that God is deserving of all our thanks for just the act of being. For creating the universe, He is worthy of our endless thanks, and that's even before we get to the part about Him clothing Himself in human flesh and dying an excruciating death for our redemption.

God is worthy of our thanks because He Is. He didn't have to "earn" our gratitude, everything he has done for us, for you and me, for all mankind, was done out of pure love; because God is love. (1 John 4:8-10)

The preface sets the table for the consecration to come, it lays the groundwork with thanks and praises to God, because it is "right and just" to praise Him "always and everywhere." (Colossians 3:17)


## THE ACCLAMATION

As the preface comes to a close, the priest invites us to join "all the angels and saints" in their unending hymn of praise.

That turn of phrase isn't just poetic language, it's not symbolic or metaphorical, we are actually joining in with the heavenly worship of all the angels and saints in heaven. Not only does this tie into the fact that the Mass is the visible earthly liturgy and a foretaste of the invisible heavenly liturgy, but also includes the Communion of Saints, our belief that all the Church is joined as one Body of Christ that can't be separated by death, because those in heaven are fully alive!

---

"In the earthly liturgy we share in a foretaste of that heavenly liturgy which is celebrated in the Holy City of Jerusalem toward which we journey as pilgrims, where Christ is sitting at the right hand of God, Minister of the sanctuary and of the true tabernacle. With all the warriors of the heavenly army we sing a hymn of glory to the Lord; venerating the memory of the saints, we hope for some part and fellowship with them; we eagerly await the Savior, our Lord Jesus Christ, until he, our life, shall appear and we too will appear with him in glory."

— (CCC 1090)

---

Even the words that we sing are the actual words of praise that are sung to the Lord for all eternity! Here they are, and they are beautiful:

---

"Holy, Holy, Holy Lord God of hosts. Heaven and earth are full of your glory. Hosanna in the highest. Blessed is he who comes in the name of the Lord. Hosanna in the highest."

— *(ROMAN MISSAL,* EUCHARISTIC PRAYER I, SANCTUS)

---

How do we know the lyrics to such a heavenly hymn? They can be found right there in the scriptures. The first portion comes from Isaiah's vision of the throne room of God.

---

"In the year that King Uzzi'ah died I saw the Lord sitting upon a throne, high and lifted up; and his train filled the temple. Above him stood the seraphim; each had six wings: with two he covered his face, and with two he covered his feet, and with two he flew. And one called to another and said: "Holy, holy, holy is the LORD of hosts; the whole earth is full of his glory."

— (ISAIAH 6:1-3)

---

Saint John heard this same song being sang by the "four living creatures" around the throne of God in Revelation (Rev 4:8).

We sing these words to affirm our belief in the holiness of God, we sing of the thrice holy God because human language and reason can't comprehend how holy God is. God's holiness can't be measured in terms that our finite minds would understand, so we use the repetition of "Holy, Holy, Holy" as superlative language to express a mystery of God. Another possible reason for the Angelic hymn to be repeated three times is a reference to Holy Trinity, not fully revealed in the Old Testament but existing from all eternity.

We also recognize that the heaven and earth are full of God's glory (Psalms 19:1). If we don't sing His praises, then Jesus tells us the rocks will cry out (Luke 19:40)

The second part of the Sanctus is from the words of the crowds on Palm Sunday, when Jesus entered Jerusalem and was hailed as the messiah. The crowds shouted these words, words that were familiar to them, they come from

THE BEAUTY OF THE MASS

Psalms 118:25-26 and were part of the Hallel Psalms that were sung during the Passover meal (Psalms 113-118).

---

"And the crowds that went before him and that followed him shouted, " Hosanna to the Son of David! Blessed is he who comes in the name of the Lord! Hosanna in the highest!"

— MATTHEW 21:9)

---

These two parts that make up this prayer are sang together and make up the acclamation portion of the Eucharistic Prayer. We acclaim, with one voice, with the Church Militant (those of us on earth), the Church Triumphant (the saints and angels in Heaven), and even the Church Suffering (the Holy souls in purgatory), that God is three incomprehensibly Holy Persons in one, and that He has come to save His people.

Hosanna means "save us," and that is the very reason that Jesus came into the world; to save us from our sins, and in fact the meaning of the name of Jesus. (Matthew 1:21)

When the people of Jerusalem called out "hosanna" when Jesus entered the city on Palm Sunday, they were crying out for God to save them, but also prophetically announcing Jesus as the One who would save all mankind.

EPICLESIS

The Epiclesis (From Greek: "calling down from on high") is the moment when the priest invokes the Holy Spirit to come upon the gifts on the altar.

This element of the prayer is very distinctive for two reasons; one, is that as soon as we finish singing the Sanctus, everyone but the priest kneels in reverence; and the other, is that the priest makes a motion with his hands that isn't made anywhere else in the liturgy. In this movement, the priest joins his hands in front of him, and then lowers them together, over top of the gifts, while praying for the Holy Spirit to descend upon them.

---

"The Epiclesis ("invocation upon") is the intercession in which the priest begs the Father to send the Holy Spirit, the Sanctifier, so that the offerings may become the body and blood of Christ and that the faithful by receiving them, may themselves become a living offering to God."

— (CCC 1105)

---

At this point, if the pastor of the parish has decided to use them, a bell may be rung. The bell comes from a time when churches were very large, very loud, and lacking in any kind of voice amplification. Sometimes the laity didn't speak Latin, and were not able to hear or follow along with what was happening in the Mass, often even praying their own prayers while the priest offered the Mass. For these reasons, the altar server would ring a small bell, here, and two other places, to call attention to the central rite, and "summit" of the entire liturgy.

---

"Make holy, therefore, these gifts, we pray by sending down your Spirit upon them like the dewfall, so that they may become for us the Body and Blood of our Lord Jesus Christ."

— (*ROMAN MISSAL*, EUCHARISTIC PRAYER II)

---

From this point, the priest transitions directly into the words of consecration.

## INSTITUTION NARRATIVE AND CONSECRATION

In this element of the prayer, we hear what is called "the institution narrative," that being the very words that Christ used when He instituted the Eucharist at the very first Mass, in the upper room on Holy Thursday, at the Last Supper.

Before the priest says the words of Christ, there is a short introduction,

---

"On the day before he was to suffer he took bread in his holy and venerable hands, and with eyes raised to heaven to you, O God, his almighty Father, giving you thanks he said the blessing, broke the bread and gave it to his disciples, saying:"

— (*ROMAN MISSAL*, EUCHARISTIC PRAYER I)

---

The words of Institution follow immediately after this introduction. People often ask when transubstantiation takes place, Saint Thomas Aquinas said that the change is affected at the last moments of the Words of Institution,

"And therefore it must be said that this change, as stated above, is wrought by Christ's words which are spoken by the priest, so that the last instant of pronouncing the words is the first instant in which Christ's body is in the sacrament..."

— (*SUMMA THEOLOGIÆ*, Q.75,A.7)

Saint John called Jesus "the Word made flesh" in the prologue of his Gospel (John 1:14), and tells us that all that exists, both visible and invisible, came into existence through His Word. God spoke the entire universe into existence (Genesis 1:3); Jesus spoke to the little girl and raised her from the dead (Mark 5:41); He used the power of His words to command Lazarus to come out of the tomb (John 11:43); and He used that same power of the Word of God, the Logos, that created all, to change the bread and wine into His Body and Blood.

We know that repeating the words that Christ said at the Last Supper, words that we call the Institution Narrative, have been part of the liturgy of the Church since the very beginning, because it is by these words that the Form of the sacrament is accomplished

The Council of Trent declared "Every Sacrament consists

of two things, matter, which is called the element, and form, which is commonly called the word."; in baptism it's the Trinitarian formula of "I baptize you in the name of The Father, Son, and Holy Spirit," and water. In the Blessed Sacrament, the matter is bread and wine, and the form is made up by the Words of Institution.

The Institution Narrative comes from the synoptic Gospels, and from Saint Paul's First letter to the Corinthians. As Saint Thomas Aquinas said, it's at the very moment these words are said, that the bread and wine cease to exist, only the accidents of bread and wine remain, and what is before us, in the hands of the priest, is truly the Body, Blood, Soul, and Divinity of Jesus Christ.

Just like Christ's divinity was always present in Him, even from the moment of His conception, but was invisible to the human senses -except for that one exceptional moment on the mount of transfiguration- so too is Jesus present before our eyes, even if we can't see Him there.

When the priest says the words of Christ, in the Institution Narrative, he is acting in Persona Christi, and we are to hear the words as if we are at the Last Supper and Jesus is saying them directly to us. The reason for this is because we are, and He is! Just as the Mass is the one sacrifice of Calvary made present, it is also a re-presentation of the Last Supper.

(Anamnesis, that is the word used by Jesus in all three synoptic Gospels when telling the disciples to 'take and eat.' This word is translated as "remembrance," but that translation falls far short of the true meaning of the word. I'm mentioning it here to show the connection with the Last Supper, but it actually makes up one of the eight elements of the Eucharistic Prayer and will be covered in depth in the next section.)

At this point, the priest lifts the Host from the altar slightly, and says these words:

---

"TAKE THIS, ALL OF YOU, AND EAT OF IT, FOR THIS IS MY BODY, WHICH WILL BE GIVEN UP FOR YOU."

— (*ROMAN MISSAL*, EUCHARISTIC PRAYER I)

---

He then holds up the consecrated Host, and if the parish uses bells, one is rung during the elevation.

After a short explanation of how Christ blessed the cup, he lifts the chalice slightly as says:

"TAKE THIS, ALL OF YOU, AND DRINK FROM IT, FOR THIS IS THE CHALICE OF MY BLOOD, THE BLOOD OF THE NEW AND ETERNAL COVENANT, WHICH WILL BE POURED OUT FOR YOU AND FOR MANY FOR THE FORGIVENESS OF SINS. DO THIS IN MEMORY OF ME."

— (*ROMAN MISSAL*, EUCHARISTIC PRAYER I)

In the same way that the Host was elevated, the priest now elevates the chalice that is now filled with the Precious Blood of Our Savior.

When Jesus commands the Apostles to "do this," what is it He wants them to do? What is the "this," that He is meaning?

To a first century Jew, the answer would be crystal clear. Jesus said His Blood would be "poured out" for the forgiveness of sins. Under the Old Testament sacrificial economy, who poured out an offering to God? It was the Aaronic priests, and by telling His Apostles to "pour out" an offering for the forgiveness of sins, Christ is telling them that they are the priests of the New Covenant! He didn't have to say, "by the way, I'm ordaining you twelve as priests," because they would've gotten the message just from the context of the words that He spoke.

## MYSTERY OF FAITH

Mystery, in the language of the Church, isn't like an episode of a detective show, it's not something that we can put our thinking caps on and solve. A mystery is a belief that is revealed by God, and understood by the Church, but not completely comprehended because it's not completely comprehensible by natural means.

---

"Great indeed, we confess, is the mystery of our religion: He was manifested in the flesh, vindicated in the Spirit, seen by angels, preached among the nations, believed on in the world, taken up in glory."

— (1 TIMOTHY 3:16)

---

Only through faith can we fully accept mysteries, and transubstantiation is the central mystery. In the eastern churches they are more content with mystery and mystical explanations of things, in the western Church we are more focused on theology in the mold of Saint Anselm, who defined theology as "faith seeking understanding." So even though the Eastern and Oriental Orthodox Churches believe in the Real Presence of Christ in the Eucharist, they prefer to leave the "how" completely with God, instead of relying on transubstantiation as an explanation.

But the Mystery of Faith isn't only referring to transubstantiation, it's referring to the entire paschal mystery, the entire life of Christ, God made flesh for our redemption.

---

"Christ's whole life is a mystery of redemption. Redemption comes to us above all through the blood of his cross, but this mystery is at work throughout Christ's entire Life..."

— (CCC 517)

---

## MEMORIAL ACCLAMATION

There are three options here, and it is left to the discretion of the celebrating priest, the most common one (in my personal experience) is the first one, but let's look at all three:

I. We proclaim your Death, O Lord, and profess your Resurrection, until you come again.

---

II. When we eat this Bread and drink this Cup, we proclaim your Death, O Lord, until you come again.

---

III. Save us, Saviour of the world, for by your Cross and Resurrection you have set us free.

---

All three are brief recitations of the Gospel message. Jesus was crucified as a sin offering on our behalf (2 Corinthians 5:21), He was raised from the dead for our justification (Romans 4:25), He gave us His flesh to sustain us (John 6), and He will return in glory to judge the living and the dead (Matthew 25:31).

ANAMNESIS

Therefore, O Lord, as we celebrate the memorial of the blessed Passion, the Resurrection from the dead, and the glorious Ascension into heaven of Christ, your Son, our Lord...

— (*ROMAN MISSAL*, EUCHARISTIC PRAYER I)

Here we re-encounter this word from the Words of Institution. Anamnesis is often translated as "remembrance," but it actually means something closer to "remembering by making present."

"The Eucharist is the memorial of Christ's Passover, the making present and the sacramental offering of his unique sacrifice in the liturgy of the Church which is his Body. In all the Eucharistic Prayers we find after the words of institution a prayer called the anamnesis or memorial."

— (CCC 1362)

This concept goes all the way back to the first Passover in

Egypt, when God instructed Moses to make this a memorial forever,

---

"The LORD said to Moses and Aaron in the land of Egypt, "This month shall be for you the beginning of months; it shall be the first month of the year for you. This day shall be for you a memorial day, and you shall keep it as a feast to the LORD; throughout your generations you shall observe it as an ordinance for ever."

— (EXODUS 12:1-2,14)

---

Later in this chapter, God tells Moses that when the children ask what makes Passover special, the sons of Israel are to remind them of what God did for them.

---

"You shall observe this rite as an ordinance for you and for your sons for ever. And when you come to the land which the LORD will give you, as he has promised, you shall keep this service. And when your children say to you, 'What do you mean by this service?' you shall say, 'It is the sacrifice of the LORD's Passover, for he passed over the houses of the sons of Israel in Egypt, when he slew the Egyptians but spared our houses.' " And the people bowed their heads and worshiped."

— (EXODUS 12:24-27)

---

This command isn't just for the people that were alive in Egypt, because God told them to observe this holiday forever, and eventually those people would die. The question is anticipated in the future, "when your children..." but the answers are given as personal, real memory, and present reality even for future generations that weren't actually there.

---

"And you shall tell your son on that day, 'It is because of what the LORD did for me when I came out of Egypt.'"

— (EXODUS 13:8)

---

But even today, 3500 years later, if you attend a Passover Seder, you will hear children ask, "Why is this night different from other nights?" You will hear the father of the household proclaim it's because of "what the LORD did for me when I came out of Egypt."

We hear this in the Church's liturgy for Easter Vigil. When the deacon sings the Exsultet:

---

"This is the night, when once you led our forebears, Israel's children, from slavery in Egypt and made them pass dry-shod through the Red Sea.

---

This is the night that with a pillar of fire banished the darkness of sin.

This is the night that even now, throughout the world, sets Christian believers apart from worldly vices and from the gloom of sin, leading them to grace and joining them to his holy ones.

This is the night, when Christ broke the prison-bars of death and rose victorious from the underworld."

(Except from the Exsultet)

This is the essence of Anamnesis. Just as the Jewish family that is celebrating the Passover are remembering and making present the events of the past, we as a Christian family are recalling and making present the events of that first Easter Vigil.

In the hundreds of times that the Old Testament uses "remember," it most often doesn't mean to just be nostalgic. It means to call to mind the past deeds of God and know that His actions are still working in the present.

---

"In the sense of Sacred Scripture, the memorial is not merely the recollection of past events, but the proclamation of the mighty works wrought by God for men. In the liturgical celebration of these events, they become in a certain way present and real. This is how Israel understands its liberation from Egypt: every time Passover is celebrated the Exodus events are made present to the memory of believers so that they may conform their lives to them."

— (CCC 1363)

---

By understanding the concept of Anamnesis, we can better grasp the miraculous re-presentation of the events of Christ's sacrifice on Calvary.

CHRIST DIED ONCE

---

"For we know that Christ being raised from the dead will never die again; death no longer has dominion over him."

— (ROMANS 6:9)

---

---

"For Christ also died for sins once for all, the righteous for the unrighteous, that he might bring us to God, being put to death in the flesh but made alive in the spirit;"

— (1 PETER 3:18)

---

One main objection against the sacrificial reality of the Mass, even since the earliest days of the Protestant reformation, is that the Church re-sacrifices Jesus at every Mass. This is not what the Church teaches, as we saw back in paragraph 1367 of the Catechism, the sacrifice of the Mass, and the sacrifice of Calvary, are one in the same. It is a miracle that we have the one sacrifice of Calvary re-presented for us to witness and participate in.

In paragraph 1366, the Catechism quotes the Council of Trent, and explains that Christ is not re-sacrificed at every Mass:

"The Eucharist is thus a sacrifice because it re-presents (makes present) the sacrifice of the cross, because it is its memorial and because it applies its fruit: [Christ], our Lord and God, was once and for all to offer himself to God the Father by his death on the altar of the cross, to accomplish there an everlasting redemption. But because his priesthood was not to end with his death, at the Last Supper "on the night when he was betrayed," [he wanted] to leave to his beloved spouse the Church a visible sacrifice (as the nature of man demands) by which the bloody sacrifice which he was to accomplish once for all on the cross would be re-presented, its memory perpetuated until the end of the world, and its salutary power be applied to the forgiveness of the sins we daily commit."

— (CCC 1366)

This is why Anamnesis is so important. We have to understand it to know that it is the sacrifice of Good Friday that we see on the altar before us, and not our Lord dying over and over, every time we celebrate the Eucharist.

(This book is not a work of apologetics, it's more of a catechesis on the liturgy, but I felt this an important topic to cover.)

## OFFERING

The Offering makes it very clear that the elements that just became the Body and Blood of Our Lord are sacrificial, and united with the sacrifice of Calvary,

"Therefore, O Lord, as we celebrate the memorial of the blessed Passion, the Resurrection from the dead, and the glorious Ascension into heaven of Christ, your Son, our Lord, we, your servants and your holy people, offer to your glorious majesty from the gifts that you have given us, this pure victim, this holy victim, this spotless victim, the holy Bread of eternal life and the Chalice of everlasting salvation.

Be pleased to look upon these offerings with a serene and kindly countenance, and to accept them, as once you were pleased to accept the gifts of your servant Abel the just, the sacrifice of Abraham, our father in faith, and the offering of your high priest Melchizedek, a holy sacrifice, a spotless victim.

— (*ROMAN MISSAL*, EUCHARISTIC PRAYER I)

---

The beginning of this element of the prayer is tied to the anamnesis of the last, because the Mass is one continuous act of worship, a single prayer to God.

We've seen many times before, that the Mass is a sacrifice, and this is where that sacrifice is offered to God, through the hands of the priest. The priest is acting once again in Persona Christi, that is to say he is acting in the person of Christ. Jesus offered Himself, as priest and victim, on the altar of the cross.

---

"But when Christ appeared as a high priest of the good things that have come, then through the greater and more perfect tent (not made with hands, that is, not of this creation) he entered once for all into the Holy Place, taking not the blood of goats and calves but his own blood, thus securing an eternal redemption. For if the sprinkling of defiled persons with the blood of goats and bulls and with the ashes of a heifer sanctifies for the purification of the flesh, how much more shall the blood of Christ, who through the eternal Spirit offered himself without blemish to God, purify your conscience from dead works to serve the living God. For Christ has entered, not into a sanctuary made with hands, a copy of the true one, but into heaven itself, now to appear in the presence of God on our behalf."

— (HEBREWS 9:11-14,24)

---

It is this same sacrifice that the priest offers to God, the same sacrifice that Christ offered on our behalf. It is the blood of the New Covenant that is poured out for us. Christ, our paschal lamb, has been sacrificed, so that we may celebrate the new Passover from death to life (see 1 Corinthians 5:7).

## INTERCESSIONS

In the intercessions, the priest prays for the person that the Mass is being offered for, for the universal Church, for the Pope and the local bishop, and for all the clergy, and finally for all the faithful departed.

St. Paul commanded us to pray unceasingly and to pray for one another (1 Thessalonians 5:17 & Ephesians 6:18). In the intercessions, the Church prays for the whole world, and thereby keeps this commandment. Everyday, in every corner of the globe, there is a priest saying Mass, and he is praying for you. Its mind blowing when you think of it that way.

## FINAL DOXOLOGY

While holding the chalice and host aloft, the priest proclaims this final doxology of the Eucharistic Prayer:

---

"Through him, and with him, and in him, O God, almighty Father, in the unity of the Holy Spirit, all glory and honor is yours, for ever and ever."

— (*ROMAN MISSAL,* EUCHARISTIC PRAYER I)

---

The elements that he holds above the altar have already been changed into the Body and Blood of Christ, and so when he says this prayer, and is looking at the chalice of the Precious Blood and the Body of Our Lord, he is saying this prayer about Him who he holds. He is holding the Body of Christ, sacrificed and broken for you, and saying that it is through this sacrifice that all glory is to the Father forever.

---

"And being found in human form he humbled himself and became obedient unto death, even death on a cross. Therefore God has highly exalted him and bestowed on him the name which is above every name, that at the name of Jesus every knee should bow, in heaven and on earth and under the earth, and every tongue confess that Jesus Christ is Lord, to the glory of God the Father."

— (PHILIPPIANS 2:8-11)

---

## THE GREAT AMEN

The Eucharistic prayer ends with the Great Amen. The word *amen* means "so be it" and we are saying amen, not just to the doxology that precede it, but to the entire Eucharistic prayer, and indeed to the whole Eucharistic liturgy.

Amen is said throughout Christian prayer, throughout the liturgy, and throughout scripture. This amen is different though, it is sung, and it is repeated three times, just like the Sanctus was earlier in the prayer. This is like an exclamation point on the doxology, and an emphatic confirmation in our belief that the elements that the priest holds above the altar may have the appearance of bread and wine, but they truly have become the Body and Blood of our Lord and Savior Jesus Christ.

---

"Jesus Christ himself is the "Amen." He is the definitive "Amen" of the Father's love for us. He takes up and completes our "Amen" to the Father: "For all the promises of God find their Yes in him. That is why we utter the Amen through him, to the glory of God": Through him, with him, in him, in the unity of the Holy Spirit, all glory and honor is yours, almighty Father, God, for ever and ever. AMEN."

— (CCC 1065)

---

THE BEAUTY OF THE MASS

Amen, Amen, Amen.

## THE COMMUNION RITE

### THE LORDS PRAYER

After the Great Amen, we all stand, and transition into the Communion Rite. We join in the great prayer that Christ taught us. In fact, this is the only prayer that Jesus taught His disciples during their three years together (as far as we know).

It always struck me as odd, that the priest says "we dare to say…" right before we pray the Lord's Prayer. But when you think on the words of the prayer, we are daring to call the Creator of the universe "Our Father." This was somewhat edgy for Jewish Christians, they saw God as Father, but in a far less familiar way than we do today, but gentile converts would most likely be shocked by this idea that the most powerful being in the universe, the one and only God of all creation, could be conversed with as "Father."

Such a concept would be unimaginable to the people accustomed to the Greek and Roman paganism of the gentiles. Their gods were cruel and petty, they had little or no care for the people who worshiped them, and only

CHARLES JOHNSTON

restrained themselves from smiting their worshipers because they brought gifts of wine and gold. But this Christian God was approachable, loving, caring, and didn't require extravagant sacrifices to satiate His hunger. He only wanted a relationship with His creation and for them to love Him. Had it not been at "our Savior's command and formed by Divine teaching" they may have rejected this idea all together.

In that light, saying that we "dare" to call God "Father" makes a lot more sense.

(The Lord's Prayer deserves more space than I can dedicate to it here, but I wrote a separate piece on it, that you can find in Appendix A at the end of this book)


SIGN OF PEACE

Jesus promised to give us "peace that surpasses all understanding," so it's fitting that the liturgy has us exchange a sign of peace while Christ is physically present on the altar in the form of the consecrated Host and the Precious Blood. It is the presence of Christ in our lives that brings peace, and it's the manifested physical presence that we recognize by sharing this sign of peace.

The words that the priest quotes, when inviting us to share in Christ's peace, come from the Gospel of John.

84

We should take a moment to explore this verse and it's deeper meaning,

---

"Peace I leave with you; my peace I give to you; not as the world gives do I give to you. Let not your hearts be troubled, neither let them be afraid."

— (JOHN 14:27)

---

Notice that Jesus makes a distinction between the peace that the world offers, and the peace that He gives.

The peace that the world offers isn't true peace, it's a momentary absence of conflict. Just look at what's commonly known as the "Pax Romana," it was a time of less war, and less conflict, but it wasn't absolute peace. The peace of the world is wrought by the strong subjugating the weak, it's brought about by force, either political force or on the battlefield. It's tenuous, it's fragile, and it's illusory. As soon as the enemies of Rome sensed weakness they invaded and sacked the city, bringing an end to the "peace" that the Roman Empire brought to the world. A peace, you will remember, that was enforced by a Roman governor, consenting to the brutal execution of a man he knew was innocent, all in the name of "keeping the peace" (See Mark 15:15 & John 19:12). Pilate was so concerned about a potential disruption of this fragile "peace" that he handed Christ over to be crucified. That's not real peace.

The peace of Christ is a peace that is unlike the peace the world offers, because it is permanent, it's robust, and it's substantially real. The peace that Christ offers is a peace that is quite literally out of this world. The peace of Christ is a peace that surpasses all understanding (Philippians 4:7).

It is also a reminder of another teaching of Christ, that we are to reconcile with our brothers before making an offering on the altar, and as we just said minutes earlier, the offering on the altar is Christ and is offered by the priest on our behalf, so we reconcile with those around us in a real and symbolic way before we approach the altar of the Lord.

---

"So if you are offering your gift at the altar, and there remember that your brother has something against you, leave your gift there before the altar and go; first be reconciled to your brother, and then come and offer your gift."

— (MATTHEW 5:23-24)

---

The Sign of Peace is also sometimes mistaken as a modern invention, because the Mass before Vatican II (The Tridentine Mass) has a sign of peace between the celebrating priest and a server, but not among parishioners. This is not the case, and we can know this because Saint Justin Martyr wrote about exchanging a "kiss of peace" before receiving the Eucharist in his *First Apology*.

## FRACTION RITE & AGNUS DEI

After the sign of peace, two simultaneous actions take place; the priest carries out the Fraction Rite, and the people sing the Agnus Dei (Latin: Lamb of God). We'll explore each, as though they were separated, but they actually are a single movement of the liturgy.

## FRACTION RITE

The priest takes the Host, he breaks it over the patten, and places a small piece in the chalice.

"Christ's gesture of breaking bread at the Last Supper, which gave the entire Eucharistic Action its name in apostolic times, signifies that the many faithful are made one body (1 Corinthians 10:17) by receiving Communion from the one Bread of

Life which is Christ, who died and rose for the salvation of the world...The priest breaks the Bread and puts a piece of the host into the chalice to signify the unity of the Body and Blood of the Lord in the work of salvation, namely, of the living and glorious Body of Jesus Christ."

— (GIRM, 83)

---

The reason he breaks the bread is twofold, one is because that is what the Gospels say Jesus did at the Last Supper (Luke 22:19), and the other is to symbolize how Our Lord's Body was broken for us.

Placing a piece of the Host into the chalice is called "commingling" and it comes from an ancient practice of the Church. Back in the earliest days of the Church, the celebration of the Eucharist was carried out by an Apostle, or by appointed successors of the Apostles who were the first bishops. When the bishop's church grew large enough that there would be multiple Eucharistic celebrations, he would appoint priests to celebrate the Eucharist.

To maintain a connection to the bishop, his liturgy, and his Apostolic succession, he would break off a small piece of consecrated Host called a Fermentum, and this would be sent out to all his priests to be commingled with the chalice at their Eucharistic celebrations.

The Pope would also send out a Fermentum to other bishops, this being a show of unity, and their acceptance showed they were in communion with the successor of Saint Peter, The Bishop of Rome.

As the Church spread, and dioceses grew much larger, and persecutions forced the Church underground, this practice fell out of use, but its legacy lives on in the Mass to this day.

The commingling of the Body and Blood of Christ has come to take on another spiritual meaning, apart from the ancient practice of Fermentum, and is seen to represent the Resurrection of Christ, when His Body and Soul were reunited in the tomb.

While he does this, the priest says in a low voice,

"May this mingling of the Body and Blood of our Lord Jesus Christ bring eternal life to us who receive it."

AGNUS DEI

While the priest is breaking the Host, and mingling it in the chalice, the congregation sings (or recites) the Agnus Dei.

---

"Lamb of God, who takes away the sins of the world, have mercy on us.

Lamb of God, who takes away the sins of the world, have mercy on us.

Lamb of God, who takes away the sins of the world, grant us peace."

---

This prayer is based partly on the words of John the Baptist in the Gospel of John, and these words are repeated verbatim by the priest a little further on in the Liturgy,

---

"The next day he saw Jesus coming toward him, and said, "Behold, the Lamb of God, who takes away the sin of the world!"

— (JOHN 1:29)

---

Jesus is our Passover Lamb, and is depicted as a Lamb by Saint John in Revelation 29 times. The reason this image of a lamb is repeated so many times in Revelation, and in our Liturgy, is because Jesus went to the altar of His Cross as the High Priest (Hebrews 5:10) and gave Himself as a sacrifice that could actually cleanse us of our sins, unlike the lambs and bulls of the Old covenant that only covered up sins (Hebrews 10).

Throughout the liturgy, just like it is throughout the New Testament, the image of the lamb that was slain is very prominent. This makes sure that the reality of Christ's sacrifice as our Passover Lamb (1 Corinthians 5:7) is enshrined in our hearts and minds.

## SILENT PRAYER OF THE PRIEST

After the singing, or recitation of the Agnus Dei, and after he finishes the Fraction Rite that takes place simultaneously, the priest prays one of two prayers quietly (sometimes not so quietly):

---

"Lord Jesus Christ, Son of the living God, who, by the will of the Father and the work of the Holy Spirit, through your death gave life to the world, free me by this, your most holy Body and Blood from all my sins and from every evil; keep me always faithful to your commandments, and never let me be parted from you."

---

Or,

---

"May the receiving of your Body and Blood, Lord Jesus Christ, not bring me to judgment and condemnation, but through your loving mercy be for me protection in mind and body and a healing remedy."

---

Behold

At this moment, the priest genuflects to show reverence to the person whose sacrifice is present on the altar. He then elevates the consecrated elements, elements that have been substantively changed from mere bread and wine, into the Body, Blood, Soul, and Divinity of our Lord Jesus Christ, and says,

---

"Behold the Lamb of God, behold him who takes away the sins of the world. Blessed are those called to the supper of the Lamb."

---

This is a conjunction of two verses of scripture. The first part are the words of Saint John the Baptist, that was also the basis for the Agnus Dei just moments ago, when he saw Jesus coming down to the Jordan river (John 1:29).

The second part comes from the Revelation of Saint John,

---

"And the angel said to me, "Write this: Blessed are those who are invited to the marriage supper of the Lamb." And he said to me, "These are true words of God."

— (REVELATION 19:9)

---

The "supper of the Lamb" that this proclamation is referring to, is not solely the eating the flesh of our Passover Lamb at Mass, it's also not only our participation in the sacrifice of Calvary, and it's not just the earthly participation in the heavenly liturgy, but it's a hopeful anticipation of being partakers in the "marriage supper of the Lamb" that is mentioned a couple verses earlier in Revelation.

---

"Let us rejoice and exult and give him the glory,

for the marriage of the Lamb has come, and his
Bride has made herself ready;"

— (REVELATION 19:7)

---

Throughout the Scriptures, both in the Old and New
Testaments, the image of God and His people, is
portrayed as a Bride and her Groom. Jesus Himself used
this imagery, and so did Saint Paul throughout his epistles. The Church is the bride of Christ, and our eternity
with Him is the great wedding feast that we have been
called to, if we persevere and remain in a state of grace
and friendship with God. If we keep our lamps filled with
oil and their wicks trimmed, we will be blessed to enter
this feast on the last day (see Matthew 25:1-13).

This "blessed are we who are called" statement is one of
the many multivalent declarations in the Mass. We are
blessed to be called to have faith in Christ and be
members of His Church; we are blessed to receive the
Eucharist and consume the Lamb of God; we are blessed
to called to partake of this heavenly feast where we will
eat the bread of life for all eternity.

A feast described by the prophet Isaiah 750 years before
the Groom took on human flesh and came to establish
His Church to be His bride. A celebration of the victory

that was won on mount Calvary, and that will be consummated on the mountains of Zion in the New Jerusalem,

---

"On this mountain the LORD of hosts will make for all peoples a feast of fat things, a feast of choice wines-of fat things full of marrow, of choice wines well refined. And he will destroy on this mountain the covering that is cast over all peoples, the veil that is spread over all nations. He will swallow up death for ever, and the Lord GOD will wipe away tears from all faces, and the reproach of his people he will take away from all the earth, for the LORD has spoken. It will be said on that day, "Behold, this is our God; we have waited for him, that he might save us. This is the LORD; we have waited for him; let us be glad and rejoice in his salvation."

— (ISAIAH 25:6-9)

---

## THE PRAYER OF THE CENTURION

---

"But the centurion answered him, "Lord, I am not

worthy to have you come under my roof; but only say the word, and my servant will be healed."

— (MATTHEW 8:8)

---

As the priest raises the Host and Chalice, the faithful pray the prayer of the centurion from the Gospels. The centurion was a righteous man according to Saint Luke's account (Luke 7:4-5) and heard of Jesus healing people so he sought Him out. But the centurion's faith was so strong that when Jesus offered to come to his house, the centurion said that he believed Jesus' words were enough to heal. This was a prophetic statement from this man, because Jesus' word is what created the universe according to the prologue of the Gospel of John.

This is the same faith that we must have when we earnestly pray the words of this faithful man. We pray his words with only the slight change of "my servant" to "my soul," and we have to realize that every time we receive the Eucharist, Christ does heal us, but although this healing isn't alway physical – though He is more than capable of healing our physical bodies if He willed it- our souls are always healed through the reception of His Body and Blood. We receive grace upon grace through this precious gift, and become more ordered to His will, and strengthened against our inclination to sin due to our fallen nature.

By consuming the flesh of Christ and asking Him to enter under the roof of our soul, we become partakers of the Divine Nature (2 Peter 1:4) and just as he transubstantiates the bread and wine into His Body and Blood, He will transform our human nature to be more like the Divine Nature.

## RECEIVING THE EUCHARIST

After we all pray the prayer of the centurion the priest gives himself communion. He, and any concelebrating priests, are the only ones who can give themselves communion. This act is called self communication and is not allowed under any other circumstances.

The reason being that the Eucharist is a gift, and the gift must be given and then received. We receive Jesus, and His Body and Blood, by the will of God, as a gift from God, and through the ministry of the Church.

As the priest consumes the Eucharist under both species, he quietly prays this prayer,

---

"May the Body of Christ keep me safe for eternal life.

May the Blood of Christ keep me safe for eternal life."

---

Just as the people of Israel were sustained in the desert by the manna that fell from heaven (Exodus 16), giving them food for the journey and nourishment to reach the promised land, we too have been given food for our souls to help us on our journey here on earth, until we reach the ultimate promised land of heaven.

The Manna that the Jews ate in the desert was bread from heaven, but it was only a foreshadowing of the Living bread from heaven. It sustained them in the desert, but it only nourished them physically, the Bread that Christ will give us, will nourish us spiritually and for all eternity. This what Jesus promised us when He told us that if we eat the "living bread come down from heaven" we would have eternal life,

---

"I am the bread of life. Your fathers ate the manna in the wilderness, and they died. This is the bread which comes down from heaven, that a man may eat of it and not die. I am the living bread which came down from heaven; if any one eats of this bread, he will live for ever; and the bread which I shall give for the life of the world is my flesh."

— (JOHN 6:48-51)

PURIFICATION OF THE VESSELS

After the reception of Holy Communion, we return to our pew and kneel in a moment of silent reflection, giving thanks for the gift He gave us in the Eucharist.

While we are praying, the priest or the deacon, is busy at the altar purifying the vessels that were used during communion. This is not just "doing the dishes" as some people call it. This is actually a very important, and very reverent part of the liturgy.

Christ is physically present in every drop of His Precious Blood that remains in the chalice, and every crumb of Host that is in the ciborium or on the patten. Because of this, and because of the reverence that is due to our King and our Creator, we should remain in a posture of reverence (usually kneeling), an attitude of reverence, and maintain a reverential silence.

The time that is used for the purification of the vessels is not a time to socialize, to check your emails, or to get up and walk out of Mass. We should behave in a way that gives the respect and honor to Our Lord, present in the Blessed Sacrament, that He deserves.

While purifying the vessels, the priest or deacon prays a beautiful and profound prayer. This prayer is very ancient, and according to some liturgical scholars, it was once a prayer that all the faithful prayed after communion,

"What has passed our lips as food, O Lord, may we possess in purity of heart, that what has been given to us in time may be our healing for eternity."

We receive the Eucharist "in time" but the sacrament's graces and highest purpose are to take us out of time and set us on a course for eternity.

# 4

## CONCLUDING RITE

The Concluding Rite is very short, and actually only consist of the Post-Communion prayer, the blessing, and the dismissal. (Technically the post communion prayer is part of the Liturgy of the Eucharist, but I've included in this chapter because most people consider it part of the Concluding Rite)

Once again, we assume the posture for prayer, standing, and join our prayer with the priest as he thanks God for the Liturgy we just celebrated. After the post-communion prayer, the priest may ask you to sit while a lector reads some parish announcements.

Once the announcements have been made- if there are any- then all rise and receive a blessing from the priest.

CHARLES JOHNSTON

Priests of God have been giving blessings all the way back to the days of Melchizedek and the Aaronic priests of the Mosaic Covenant, and so we today receive a parting blessing from our priests who offer the sacrifice of the Mass on our behalf.

## DISMISSAL

The Mass has many names, the catechism (CCC 1328-1332) lists a few different terms that we may call this Liturgical aspect of the life of the Church, but Mass is the most common one in the western church. The dismissal is actually where we get the term "Mass" from. Ite, missa est is how the priest would dismiss the faithful in the Tridentine Mass, with "missa" being Anglicized into "Mass". This roughly translates as "Go, it (the assembled faithful) is dismissed," but Pope Benedict XVI wrote how there can be a deeper meaning to these simple words of dismissal,

"After the blessing, the deacon or the priest dismisses the people with the words: Ite, missa est. These words help us to grasp the relationship between the Mass just celebrated and the mission of Christians in the world. In antiquity, missa

102

simply meant "dismissal." However, in Christian usage it gradually took on a deeper meaning. The word "dismissal" has come to imply a "mission." These few words succinctly express the missionary nature of the Church. The People of God might be helped to understand more clearly this essential dimension of the Church's life, taking the dismissal as a starting- point."

— (*SACRAMENTUM CARITATIS*, 51)

---

We are sent on a missio, a mission, and that is to live out our baptismal promises every hour of every day. We are to live as Catholic Christians at all times, and not just for the 60-90 minutes that we are in Mass on Sunday.

This is a lifetime commitment, and by being dismissed we are just getting started. Sunday is the first day of the week, and what better way to get the week started then by being sent on a mission by the Church to win souls for the Kingdom, to break down the strongholds of the enemy. Christ promised us that the "Gates of hell will not prevail" against His Church, but gates are a defensive measure, not offensive weapons. We are supposed to take the fight to the enemy, and not sit back and wait for his attack. Let's leave Mass and take the fight for souls right to the gates of hell, let's go on our mission and be an evangelical and missionary Church in our cities and countries. Let's be dismissed from Mass, to live even more authentically Catholic lives that we arrived with.

Our mission is to be saints, and to make saints around us, through our words and deeds.

THE MASS HAS ENDED

# 5

# FINAL THOUGHTS

## DON'T TAKE IT FOR GRANTED

This has been a labor of love, I love the liturgy of the Church, and I love all my readers, who I hope will have a deeper appreciation of the liturgy after reading this book, and seeing the multivalent meaning of all the actions and words of the Mass. My prayer is that this time you all have spent reading this will be spiritually rewarding and strengthening for your relationship with our Lord Jesus Christ and His Church.

What a glorious opportunity we have, to be present at the Lord's Supper, at the Supper of the Lamb, every time we go to Mass. Don't ever take that for granted, and don't let it become just a routine.

As Saint Padre Pio said, "It would be easier for the world to survive without the sun than to do so without the Holy Mass.

## AN OPPORTUNITY FOR ENCOUNTER

"Christianity is not an intellectual system, a collection of dogmas, or a moralism. Christianity is instead an encounter, a love story, an event."

— POPE BENEDICT XVI

Pope Benedict XVI said that Christianity is all about an encounter with Jesus Christ, an we can encounter Him in many ways, but most tangibly in the Mass. We hear Christ preached in the Gospel, we converse with our Lord in prayer, and we receive Him in the Blessed Sacrament. I'd encourage everyone reading this book to not see the Mass as just a "thing we do as Catholics," but to see it for what it truly is; a place to encounter Christ.

Keeping this idea of encountering Christ in the liturgy, we must always remember where we are meeting Him; we are standing at the foot of the cross on Calvary. We are present at that pivotal moment in history. We are there because the Mass is a sacrifice, the Mass is THE sacrifice, the one sacrifice of our Lord and Savior, Jesus Christ. If we keep these two things in mind, we will never take the Mass for granted.

## THE TODAH SACRIFICE

I constantly stressed, throughout this book, and whenever I discuss the liturgy, that the Mass is a sacrifice. The Mass "completes and surpasses all the sacrifices of the Old Covenant" (CCC 1330), but it isn't just a sacrifice for our sanctification like the Passover Lamb or the Yom Kippur sin offering, it is also a sacrifice of thanksgiving.

Eucharistia (Greek: "thanksgiving") is the name we commonly call the Blessed sacrament, but the celebration of the Eucharist is also a name we call the Mass. The Mass is a thanksgiving celebration for the whole of salvation, for the graces He gives us, for the very existence of the universe. God has given us so many things, and the very least we can do is to give Him thanks.

The Old Testament had a sacrifice that was prescribed for thanksgiving, known as the Todah (Hebrew: "thanks") offering, it was a subset of the peace offerings, and was the only type of sacrifice where a non-priest would partake of the sacrificial meal.

"And this is the law of the sacrifice of peace offerings which one may offer to the LORD. If he offers it for a thanksgiving, then he shall offer with the thank offering unleavened cakes mixed with oil, unleavened wafers spread with oil, and cakes of fine flour well mixed with oil. And the flesh of the sacrifice of his peace offerings for thanksgiving shall be eaten on the day of his offering; he shall not leave any of it until the morning."

— (LEVITICUS 7:11-12,15)

This sacrifice was to be offered in thanksgiving for specific events, and especially after your life was saved from certain death or grave injuries. Christ saved us by redeeming us from the death we were condemned to by the disobedience of Adam (Romans 5:17), thus the offering of a Todah sacrifice is a reasonable response.

So in essence, a Todah sacrifice was given after being saved from death (Christ on the Cross), and it was made of a Lamb (Jesus is the true Lamb), bread (Jesus is the true Bread from heaven), and is eaten by both the priest and the lay people. That sure sounds like the Mass to me! That is true Eucharistia.

There is a Midrash (ancient Rabbinical teaching on the Torah) that says, "In the time to come {the messianic age}, all sacrifices will be annulled - but the sacrifice of thanksgiving {todah} will not be annulled" (*Vayikra Rabbah* 9:7). The "age to come," or messianic age, is the times we are currently living in, but that the Jewish people still await. The Midrash says that all sacrifices would cease to be offered, except for the Todah sacrifice. That sacrifice would continue for eternity. The Temple in Jerusalem was destroyed by General Titus in 70AD, thus ending all sacrifices, but our sacrifice of thanksgiving has been offered to God every day, and on ever corner of the globe since the days of the Apostles.

## WE MUST PARTICIPATE

I'd like to finish this book with a couple of paragraphs from one of the Constitutions from the Second Vatican Council, it stresses the importance of the liturgy in the life of the Church, but even more importantly, it stresses the importance of our full, active, and conscious participation in this sacred liturgy.

As I've said before, we can't fully, actively, and consciously participate in something without a basic understanding of what it is. We can't engage in the prayerful participation in the Mass that the council fathers called for, unless we take the initiative to learn more about our faith and the liturgical life of the Church.

---

"Nevertheless the liturgy is the summit toward which the activity of the Church is directed; at the same time it is the font from which all her power flows. For the aim and object of apostolic works is that all who are made sons of God by faith and baptism should come together to praise God in the midst of His Church, to take part in the sacrifice, and to eat the Lord's supper."

---

The liturgy in its turn moves the faithful, filled with "the paschal sacraments," to be "one in holiness";it prays that "they may hold fast in their lives to what they have grasped by their faith";the renewal in the Eucharist of the covenant between the Lord and man draws the faithful into the compelling love of Christ and sets them on fire. From the liturgy, therefore, and especially from the Eucharist, as from a font, grace is poured forth upon us; and the sanctification of men in Christ and the glorification of God, to which all other activities of the Church are directed as toward their end, is achieved in the most efficacious possible way.

But in order that the liturgy may be able to produce its

full effects, it is necessary that the faithful come to it with proper dispositions, that their minds should be attuned to their voices, and that they should cooperate with divine grace lest they receive it in vain. Pastors of souls must therefore realize that, when the liturgy is celebrated, something more is required than the mere observation of the laws governing valid and licit celebration; it is their duty also to ensure that the faithful take part fully aware of what they are doing, actively engaged in the rite, and enriched by its effects."

(*Sacrosanctum Concilium*, 10 & 11)

Since our relationship with Christ should be the most important relationship in our lives; and since the Mass is where we most intimately experience and encounter with Him, through prayer, hearing His Word, and consuming His glorified flesh; then attending and participating in the Mass is the most important and meaningful thing we will ever do in this life. Please don't let it become just your Sunday morning routine.

# 6

# APPENDIX A

## THE LORD'S PRAYER

What is the Perfect Prayer? Any time you speak to God from your heart and remain in reverent silence to allow Him to speak to you, I'd say that's a pretty good start.

We sometimes forget that prayer isn't a one-way street, it isn't giving God a list of demands and then hanging up the phone. We have to remember that prayer isn't a hostile negotiation, it's a conversion in the context of a relationship. We have to approach God and speak with Him, not at Him.

But what about those times when we don't really know what to say, or there's a longing that we wish to express but just can't find the right words? For these, and many other situations, I can't think of a better way to pray than with the words our Savior gave us.

Some people say that Christ was only giving us a template of how to pray, but never intended to show us what to pray. I agree that the Lord's Prayer is the perfect template for prayer but disagree that Christ didn't intend for us to use His words when praying. In this prayer is the full perfection of prayer, from adoration, to contrition, petition, and praise.

The structure and rhythm of the *Our Father,* or *Lord's Prayer,* as it's often called, is as close to perfection as can be. First of all, it was dictated to the Apostles, and through Sacred Scripture to us, by the Son of God Himself. Also, it puts our petitions and praises into proper perspective and order. It doesn't start by asking anything of God, it begins by praising His Holy Name.

We've all prayed this prayer many times over, even when I was a child at Presbyterian churches, it was part of the Liturgy, but let's slow it down and look at each line by itself and study the perfect prayer from the perfect Son of God.

It is recognized that there are seven petitions in the prayer; three are ordered towards God, and four are ordered towards us. We pray this prayer as an individual, but we also pray it as a unified people of God and petition Him on behalf of all believers in all places. To reinforce the fact that Christianity is a family affair, and not an individualistic one, this pray is prayed as a group, even if you are alone in your home, you are still praying it with everyone that calls God "Father."

OUR FATHER, WHO ART IN HEAVEN

While not counted as one of the seven petitions of the prayer, the way it is addressed to a familiar father, and not to a far off, distant God, sets the tone for the prayer to come.

---

"Many religions invoke God as "Father". The deity is often considered the "father of gods and of men." In Israel, God is called "Father" inasmuch as he is Creator of the world. Even more, God is Father because of the covenant and the gift of the law to Israel, "his first-born son." God is also called the Father of the king of Israel. Most especially he is "the Father of the poor", of the orphaned and the widowed, who are under his loving protection."

— (CCC 238)

---

The image of God as Father wasn't unheard of in Jesus' day, the Jews of His time recognized God as the Father and creator of all things. They also saw Him as the Father of the people of Israel. But the way that Jesus refers to God as Father in all of His prayers, and all His teachings, really rubbed the authorities the wrong way. They thought Jesus was being overly familiar, and far too informal with the One True God. They also understood that if God was the father of Jesus, that would make Jesus equal with the Father, and that was unacceptable to them.

"This was why the Jews sought all the more to kill him, because he not only broke the sabbath but also called God his Father, making himself equal with God."

— (JOHN 5:18)

Jews had, and still have to this day, a great reverence for God. So much so that they refuse to pronounce His name, except for on the most solemn occasions. Their relationship with God was one of Lord and serf, while Jesus was showing His apostles that we can have a Father and child relationship with the living God. We can approach God as a child approaches their parent, without formality, just simply and familiarly.

When we say that God is "in heaven," it doesn't mean we are saying that God is in anyway limited to a particular point in space, or even that heaven itself is a location. God is omnipresent, meaning He is everywhere at once, but Saint Augustine read this line to mean "in the hearts of the righteous, as it were in His holy temple."

Heaven is not a physical realm, it is a spiritual reality. So, to reach God with our prayers we must enter into this spiritual reality, just like Jesus told the Samaritan woman,

"God is spirit, and those who worship him must worship in spirit and truth."

— (JOHN 4:24)

We must reach out not just with words, but with our heart and soul, and that is where we will meet God. In the hearts of the righteous is where God "is."

## HALLOWED BE THY NAME

In this line we are recognizing the Holiness of the Name of God. The word "hallowed" is not meant to say that we are causing His Name to be Holy, but we are only acknowledging its holiness.

God's name is to be held in such high regard that we are not to say it without good reason. We are to keep it Holy and not take it in vain, as God told Moses in the Ten Commandments. (Exodus 20:7)

---

"Among all the words of Revelation, there is one which is unique: the revealed name of God. God confides his name to those who believe in him; he reveals himself to them in his personal mystery. The gift of a name belongs to the order of trust and intimacy. "The Lord's name is holy." For this reason, man must not abuse it. He must keep it in mind in silent, loving adoration. He will not introduce it into his own speech except to bless, praise, and glorify it."

— (CCC 2143)

---

The People of Israel, from back during the Old Covenant, and to the Jews of today, avoid saying the divine name, even during liturgical readings of the Torah. They replaced the Tetragrammaton (YHWH) with *"Adonai"* which means "Lord." In keeping with this translational tradition, in many modern bibles you may see "LORD" substituted where the Tetragrammaton would've been in the original manuscripts.

This was the way they interpreted the Second Commandment. To not take the Lord's name in vain, meant to not say it at all. This isn't the way the Church interprets the Second Commandment, but by this act of reverence, we can appreciate how seriously they took the words spoken to Moses on Mount Sinai. We should endeavor to treat God's Holy Name with such respect, and especially the name of His Son. The name of Jesus is the "Name above all names" (Philippians 2:9), it should not be said so flippantly as society uses it today and should never be used as a profanity. To use the name of Jesus in such a way is a direct violation of the Second Commandment and a form of blasphemy.

The first petition of the Lord's Prayer reminds us of all these principles in a few simple words; "Hallowed be Thy Name"

THY KINGDOM COME

The second petition has us praying for the coming of God's Kingdom.

---

"Jesus' entry into Jerusalem manifests the coming

of the kingdom that the Messiah-King, welcomed into his city by children and the humble of heart, is going to accomplish by the Passover of his Death and Resurrection."

— (CCC 570)

---

Both Jesus and John the Baptist said that "the Kingdom of God is at hand" (Matthew 3:2 & Mark 1:15). The Kingdom of God is currently found in the Church that He established and left on this earth to be a light unto the nations and a herald of the Gospel. This Kingdom is the shining city on a hill (Matthew 5:14) that is a beacon to salvation for all the world.

But the Kingdom is also a future reality. We say in the Creed every Sunday, that Christ will come to judge the living and the dead, and it is at this final coming of Christ that He will establish His Kingdom in all its fullness for all eternity.

It's this coming Kingdom that we all look forward to, it's in this Kingdom that God will rule His people for all time. By praying this petition, we are saying, with all the saints throughout history, "come Lord" (Rev 22:17)

## THY WILL BE DONE ON EARTH AS IT IS IN HEAVEN

Seeking for God's will to be done should always be part of our prayers. It should be our highest desire to do God's will, because God's will is all good, all just, and all holy. By conforming ourselves to His perfect will, we make ourselves more holy, and personal holiness is the goal of all Catholics. We are called to be saints, and saints do the will of God.

---

"By prayer we can discern "what is the will of God" and obtain the endurance to do it. Jesus teaches us that one enters the kingdom of heaven not by speaking words, but by doing "the will of my Father in heaven.""

— (CCC 2826)

---

But what about this clause, "as it is in Heaven"? In Heaven, we will be in complete union with God's perfect will, no longer encumbered by concupiscence or the cares of this world, we will perform His will without question and without hesitation.

To pray that His will be done "on earth as it is in Heaven," is essentially to ask that we be more conformed to His will, just like the Saints in Heaven. That His will be carried out by His servants here on earth, like the commands of a king are carried out by his loyal soldiers.

We don't have to wait, we shouldn't wait, until we are in Heaven to conform ourselves to God's will, and to carry it out here on earth. We are God's loyal soldiers as members of the Church Militant. Let's pray this petition with all our heart, and endeavor to do God's will at all time.

This petition is manifested in the Feast of Christ the King. The encyclical that was promulgated by Pope Pius XI to establish this feast, sums up how Christ is to reign as sovereign King on earth as He already does in heaven.

To truly pray this petition means to truly submit to the kingship of Christ, and not just metaphorically, but in the realest sense. It means to wholly, completely, and without question, submit yourself to the will and sovereignty of God.

---

"It has long been a common custom to give to Christ the metaphorical title of "King," because of the high degree of perfection whereby he excels all creatures. So, he is said to reign "in the hearts of men," both by reason of the keenness of his intellect and the extent of his knowledge, and also because he is very truth, and it is from him that truth must be obediently received by all mankind. He reigns, too, in the wills of men, for in him the human will was perfectly and entirely obedient to the Holy Will of God, and further by his grace and inspiration he so subjects our free-will as to incite us to the most noble endeavors. He is King of hearts, too, by reason of his "charity which exceedeth all knowledge." And his mercy and kindness which draw all men to him, for never has it been known, nor will it ever be, that man be loved so much and so universally as Jesus Christ. But if we ponder this matter more deeply, we cannot but see that the title and the power of King belongs to Christ as man in the strict and proper sense too. For it is only as man that he may be said to have received from the Father "power and glory and a kingdom," since the Word of God, as consubstantial with the Father, has all things in common with him, and therefore has necessarily supreme and absolute dominion over all things created."

— (*QUAS PRIMAS*, 7)

## GIVE US THIS DAY OUR DAILY BREAD

"Give us"

By baptism we are adopted children of God, and as His children we have the right to request from Him our sustenance. Just as a child lives off of the food provided by his father, so too do we survive from the food, both physically and spiritual, that is given to us by our Father in Heaven.

"This Day"

This is the recognition that every day is a gift from God, and that we survive on a daily basis because of His divine benevolence. The entire universe is held in existence by His nature of existence, and because of His will. Each day we are taken care of if we allow ourselves to rely on His grace.

---

"Have no anxiety about anything, but in everything by prayer and supplication with thanksgiving let your requests be made known to God."

— (PHILIPPIANS 4:6)

---

## "Our Daily Bread"

We may interpret this as "that sustenance with which we survive each day" or another variation of asking God to provide for our physical needs. In the literal sense of the text, this is a very good interpretation of what is being prayed. We need to have faith that God will supply all our needs, and not to worry about even basic things for survival, like bread.

> "Therefore I tell you, do not be anxious about your life, what you shall eat or what you shall drink, nor about your body, what you shall put on. Is not life more than food, and the body more than clothing? Look at the birds of the air: they neither sow nor reap nor gather into barns, and yet your heavenly Father feeds them. Are you not of more value than they? And which of you by being anxious can add one cubit to his span of life?"
>
> — (MATTHEW 6:25-27)

Even though this is the literal sense of the text, I don't believe it should be how we primarily read and pray it. Not long before Jesus taught the disciples this prayer, He had said to the Devil,

"It is written, 'Man shall not live by bread alone, but by every word that proceeds from the mouth of God.'"

— (MATTHEW 4:4)

Jesus said "it is written" so, that should make us look to where it is written, and what was the context of that passage.

The passage that Jesus is quoting, comes to us from Deuteronomy and in it, Moses is reminding the people of Israel of all the things God has done for them. One of these things is that He has fed them with both Manna and the Word that has come from His mouth.

"And he humbled you and let you hunger and fed you with manna, which you did not know, nor did your fathers know; that he might make you know that man does not live by bread alone, but that man lives by everything that proceeds out of the mouth of the LORD."

— (DEUTERONOMY 8:3)

Manna was the miraculous "bread that came down from heaven," and is a type and prefigurement of the Eucharist.

---

"Yet he commanded the skies above and opened the doors of heaven; and he rained down upon them manna to eat and gave them the bread of heaven. Man ate of the bread of the angels; he sent them food in abundance."

— (PSALM 78:23-25)

---

Jesus tells the Jews in John 6, that even though their fathers ate this "bread of Angels," as the Psalmist called it, they still died. The bread that kept the Israelites alive for 40 years, although miraculous was still only a shadow, a sign, of the true Bread of Life. Jesus is the Bread of Life, and this Bread does not perish, like the manna that couldn't be kept even overnight, but it "endures to eternal life." (John 6:27)

---

"I am the bread of life. Your fathers ate the manna in the wilderness, and they died. This is the bread which comes down from heaven, that a man may eat of it and not die. I am the living bread which came down from heaven; if any one eats of this bread, he will live for ever; and the bread which I shall give for the life of the world is my flesh."

— (JOHN 6:48-51)

But Moses told them that it wasn't the bread alone that sustained them in the desert, it was also "every word that proceeds from the mouth of the LORD." This is another clue in the typological message of the Old Testament, a clue that points directly to Jesus and the Eucharist.

What was it that John the Evangelist called Jesus in the opening line of the prologue of his Gospel?

"In the beginning was the Word, and the Word was with God, and the Word was God."

— (JOHN 1:1)

The Israelites were sustained by eating the "bread of Angels" and hearing the Word of God, how much more are we blessed to be able to consume the Word of God, and the Bread of Life in the Blessed Sacrament.

This is what we are praying for in this petition of the prayer, we are praying to be sustained by the Eucharist and by eating His Flesh, and drinking His Blood, that we may be fed by Him until He comes to take us home.

Another interesting thing about this petition, is that it contains a word that is found nowhere else in scripture. This word is *"Epiousios,"* and is usually translated as "daily" in English. But this falls far short of what this word actually says. It's a conjunction of two Greek words, *epi* meaning above or beyond, and *ousia* meaning substance. Put together, it is best translated as "super-substantial" or "above-substance," or "that which is above normal substance of bread."

Now looking back at what else we've discovered about this petition in the prayer, what else could be "super-substantial" bread than the Eucharist?

---

"The Fathers of the Church were practically unanimous in understanding the fourth petition of the Our Father (Lord's Prayer) as a Eucharistic petition."

— (BENEDICT XVI, JESUS OF
NAZARETH)

---

AND FORGIVE US OUR TRESPASSES, AS WE
FORGIVE THOSE WHO TRESPASS AGAINST US

The fifth petition is the only one that carries a contingency clause. Our forgiveness from God is directly contingent on our forgiveness towards others. (See CCC 2838)

This isn't a suggestion, it is a binding commandment, upon which our own forgiveness hinges. If we refuse to forgive others, God will refuse to forgive us. It actually is that black and white.

---

"For if you forgive men their trespasses, your Heavenly Father also will forgive you; but if you do not forgive men their trespasses, neither will your Father forgive your trespasses."

— (MATTHEW 6:14-15)

---

These words of Christ immediately follow His teaching the disciples the Lord's Prayer. He says "if" you forgive, this is because the Lord knows that many will refuse to forgive others, and thus exclude themselves from His loving forgiveness. Just as the "unforgivable sin"

(Matthew 12:30-32) is believed to be final impenitence, and excluding yourself from God's covenant with all mankind, so too is it with those who refuse God's forgiveness because they prefer to continue not forgiving others.

---

"And whenever you stand praying, forgive, if you have anything against any one; so that your Father also who is in heaven may forgive you your trespasses."

— (MARK 11:25)

---

(See also the parable of the wicked servant Matthew 18:23-35)

## AND LEAD US NOT INTO TEMPTATION

In this petition, are we asking God not to tempt us with sin? Of course not. God doesn't lead us to temptation, while we beg him not to. Although that is an all too common misconception about this line in the prayer.

"This petition goes to the root of the preceding one, for our sins result from our consenting to temptation; we therefore ask our Father not to "lead" us into temptation. It is difficult to translate the Greek verb used by a single English word: the Greek means both "do not allow us to enter into temptation" and "do not let us yield to temptation." "God cannot be tempted by evil and he himself tempts no one"; on the contrary, he wants to set us free from evil. We ask him not to allow us to take the way that leads to sin. We are engaged in the battle "between flesh and spirit"; this petition implores the Spirit of discernment and strength."

— (CCC 2846)

St James makes it clear and is quoted in the above paragraph from the catechism, that we are never tempted by God, and that if we give into temptation, it leads to sin, and sin, ultimately leads to death.

"Let no one say when he is tempted, "I am tempted by God"; for God cannot be tempted with evil and he himself tempts no one; but each person is tempted when he is lured and enticed by his own desire. Then desire when it has conceived gives birth to sin; and sin when it is full-grown brings forth death."

— (JAMES 1:13-15)

---

This petition is recognizing that a child of God should put their life into His divine providence in such a way, that He leads us in all we do, and in everywhere we go. It also asks that He lead us into His will, and conform our will to His, so that we do not fall into temptation that we would otherwise face, if we were going after our own desires.

We are given free will, and the decision to surrender ourselves to God, and His plans, is entirely free, but it's only by the grace of God that we could even make such a choice to abandon ourselves to divine providence.

The catechism states, that to surrender to His will is actually a great victory, and a victory only possible through prayer (CCC 2849).

By praying to be able to abandon ourselves to His will, we are actively decreasing ourselves so that He may increase in us. Just as John the Baptist said, "He must increase, but I must decrease." (John 3:30) So that we can say as Saint Paul said, "it is no long i who live, but Christ who lives in me." (Galatians 2:20)

We May find ourselves in difficult circumstances, and we may be tempted to choose the wrong path, but by the grace of God, we ask that He take us by the hand, like the children we are, and lead us to His path.

## BUT DELIVER US FROM EVIL

Delivery from evil, and its primary agent; that is essentially what the Gospel is all about. We are delivered, by the life, death, and resurrection of Jesus, from the evils we have chosen. We were born with original sin, but have also chosen sin throughout our lives, and only by Christ's atoning sacrifice can we be delivered.

Our first parents were deceived by the evil one, and they fell from friendship with God. Now that we have a channel, by which we can restore that lost friendship and innocence, we ask that God protect us from the evil one so that we may not fall again.

---

"In this petition, evil is not an abstraction, but refers to a person, Satan, the Evil One, the angel who opposes God. The devil (dia-bolos) is the one who "throws himself across" God's plan and his work of salvation accomplished in Christ."

— (CCC 2851)

---

By placing ourselves within His will, and asking to be kept from the evil one, we are petitioning the Lord to keep us in a state of grace, so that when we reach the end of this life, we will see Him face to face in the heavenly Kingdom.

---

"Deliver us, Lord, we beseech you, from every evil and grant us peace in our day, so that aided by your mercy we might be ever free from sin and protected from all anxiety, as we await the blessed hope and the coming of our Savior, Jesus Christ."

— (*ROMAN MISSAL*, EMBOLISM AFTER THE LORD'S PRAYER)

---

Amen

(Adapted from a post on my website nowthatim-catholic.com

When I first set out to write this post, I was unaware that there is an entire section of the catechism dealing with the Lord's Prayer. I used these paragraphs liberally throughout, they are CCC 2803-2854 and can be found here http://www.vatican.va/archive/ccc_css/archive/catechism/p4s2a3.htm )

# APPENDIX B

## THE FOUR MARKS OF THE CHURCH

We say it every Sunday, when we rise after the homily to make our profession of faith, "I believe in one, holy, catholic, and apostolic church." These are the four marks of the Church, they were added to the Nicene creed by the First Council of Constantinople in 381AD, but their principles go back to the age of the Apostles. We all say the words, but how many of us have stopped to think about their meaning?

---

"This is the sole Church of Christ, which in the Creed we profess to be one, holy, catholic and apostolic. "These four characteristics, inseparably linked with each other, indicate essential features of the Church and her mission. The Church does not possess them of herself; it is Christ who, through the Holy Spirit, makes his Church one, holy, catholic, and apostolic, and it is He who calls her to realize each of these qualities."

— (CCC 811)

---

## ONE

(See CCC 813-822)

Jesus founded one Church, and this Church was built on St. Peter,

---

"And I tell you, you are Peter, and on this rock I will build my Church, and the gates of Hades shall not prevail against it. I will give you the keys of the kingdom of heaven, and whatever you bind on earth shall be bound in heaven, and whatever you loose on earth shall be loosed in heaven."

— (MATTHEW 16:18-19)

---

The early church was united in mission, and although they had to overcome cultural and linguistic differences, they were still one. As Saint Paul wrote in his letter to the Ephesians, "There is one body and one Spirit, just as you were called to the one hope that belongs to your call, one Lord, one faith, one baptism, one God and Father of us all, who is above all and through all and in all." (Ephesians 4:4-6) and in his letter to the Galatians,

"There is neither Jew nor Greek, there is neither slave nor free, there is neither male nor female; for you are all one in Christ Jesus."

— (GALATIANS 3:28)

The theme of unity, and oneness, runs powerfully throughout the Pauline epistles. By reading through the New Testament, it becomes obvious that although the churches were separated by geography, language, and cultures, they were all one Church.

This becomes very evident when a dispute between Gentile and Hebrew Christians arose, There was a general council called in Jerusalem to sort it out. Recorded in Acts 15, the church of Jerusalem sent a letter to Antioch, a city outside of Roman Palestine and about 500 miles away (no small distance today, never mind 2000 years ago). The fact that the council in Jerusalem laid out how Jews and Gentiles were to coexist peacefully in Antioch shows how unified the church as a whole was.

Jesus also prayed in the garden of Gethsemane that His Church would be one,

---

"I do not pray for these only, but also for those who believe in me through their word, that they may all be one; even as you, Father, are in me, and I in you, that they also may be in us, so that the world may believe that you have sent me."

— (JOHN 17:20-21)

---

Division in the Body

Today Christianity is most definitely divided in many places, and lacking the oneness that Christ prayed for. There are over 2 billion Christians in the world, 1.2 billion belonging to the Catholic Church, around 900 million Protestants, 300 million Eastern Orthodox, approximately 90 million Oriental Orthodox, and millions of others that aren't easily classified.

If you break each main group down it gets even more splintered, just in Protestantism alone there are said to be over 35,000 different denominations, the majority of which are not in communion with each other and are sometimes openly hostile to each other.

Even in the orthodox communion there is great divisions, which each patriarch of all the autocephalous churches an authority unto himself. Although the orthodox churches retained a hierarchical episcopate, much like the Catholic Church that they separated from in the Great Schism of 1054, they have no unity amongst their respective leaders. Every autocephalous church (Russian orthodox, Greek Orthodox, Romanian, Bulgarian, etc.) has a bishop called a patriarch, with the patriarch of Constantinople being recognized as "the first among equals," but this is little more than an honorific title and carries hardly any real weight with the other patriarchs.

The unity of the Catholic Church

The lack of unity, in even an apostolic organization like the orthodox communion shows the need of the Petrine office (the Papacy) as integral to the unity of the church. It is the Papacy that is the glue that holds all the bishops of the Catholic Church together, he is the rock on which the church is built, and the foundation of Saint Peter was Christ Himself.

Most people think of the Catholic Church as the Roman Catholic Church, but the Wester Church, sometimes called the Latin Church (of which the Roman Rite is the largest Rite), in contrast with the Greek East, is just one of 24 churches within the Catholic Church as a whole. The Latin Church is by far the largest but is in no way "more Catholic" than our Easter Catholic brothers. It is this beautiful diversity, but still remaining in communion with each other, and this One Church, that is the greatest witness to the oneness that has persevered in the Catholic Church.

For almost 2000 years, through hundreds of great pontiffs, and more than a few bad ones, the Church has survived the divisions that has plagued the other branches of Christianity who separated themselves from the unifying force of the bishop of Rome.

Separate but still one

Although historical animosity, schism, heresy, and all manor of other scandals has split over 1 billion Christians from the church that Christ founded, we are all still one.

As we say, later in the Nicene Creed, "I believe in one baptism," and Saint Paul says, "one Lord, one faith, one baptism" (Ephesians 4:5) this means not only can you be baptized just once, but also that there is one baptism in the Lord. Essentially all validly baptized Christians (with water, and in the name of The Father, The Son, and The Holy Spirit) are baptized into the body of Christ.

We may have the separations that have crept in, and we may have different views of eschatology and ecclesiology, but we are all members of the Body of Christ, sometimes in an imperfect manor. To use the analogy of the body; even if your foot is injured, it is still a part of you.

---

"Baptism constitutes the foundation of communion among all Christians, including those who are not yet in full communion with the Catholic Church: "For men who believe in Christ and have been properly baptized are put in some, though imperfect, communion with the Catholic Church. Justified by faith in Baptism, [they] are incorporated into Christ; they therefore have a right to be called Christians, and with good reason are accepted as brothers by the children of the Catholic Church." "Baptism therefore constitutes the sacramental bond of unity existing among all who through it are reborn."

— (CCC 1271)

---

It is through our common baptism, that all Christians

share in, no matter how imperfectly, the unity and oneness of the Church. So, whenever we pray the Nicene Creed and profess the oneness of our faith, thank God for the gift of unity, and pray for those not yet in communion with us, that God may heal all the wounds that separate His children and pilgrims on earth from each other.

HOLY

(See CCC 823-829)

The Source of Holiness

It must be noted that the source of the holiness of the Church is not the members of the Church themselves, but it is Christ, who as the head of the Church is the source of its holiness.

Saint Paul, in his letter to the Collosians says,

"He is the head of the body, the Church; He is the beginning, the first-born from the dead, that in everything He might be pre-eminent."

— (COLLOSIANS 1:18)

The Church was also founded by Christ, as He told Saint

Peter, "on this rock I'll build My Church..." (Matthew 16:18) since Christ is the man without sin, and the Lamb who is called thrice Holy in Revelation, His body is also Holy. As we know the church is the body of Christ and He is its head.

St Augustine also said that as we are the Body of Christ and Christ is the head (Col 1:8), the Holy Spirit is the soul of the Church.

The *Catechism* says, quoting St Augustine,

---

"What the soul is to the human body, the Holy Spirit is to the Body of Christ, which is the Church."

— (CCC 797)

---

If Christ is the head, and the Holy Spirit is the soul, the proximity of the Church would inherit this holiness. Just as touching a leper made someone unclean, yet Jesus touched the lepers and wasn't defiled by them; He transmitted His righteousness and holiness into them, so too He transmits his holiness and righteousness into His Body that remains here on earth.

Members of The Church Can't Diminish This Mark

So, we see that the Church is Holy, not because the people who make up the Church are themselves holy, but often times in spite of them. The Church is made up of people, and as any person knows, people are sinners, but our fallen nature does not taint the nature of the Church as holy. Just as the lepers didn't taint the nature of Christ, neither can we.

Some may point to less than holy popes and bishops from centuries past, but just as sinful popes are proof of the charism of infallibility (even bad popes didn't teach heresy), so too do they prove the holiness of the Church as an institution.

Kings of Judah

If you consider that the Church is the "Israel of God," (Galations 6:16) then the comparison between the Church and Old Testament Israel is very apt, in fact it's a comparison made by many of the church fathers, theologians, and teachers throughout history on a wide range of subjects.

A parallel can be drawn between the royal descendants of King David and the Church. God promised that King David's descendants would be kings of Israel forever, this promise was fulfilled by Christ being born of the lineage of King David, and Pontius Pilate recognized (although he meant it in a mocking way, it was nevertheless prophetic) Jesus as "King of the Jews."

If you read through the history of the Kings of the United Israel, and after the kingdom was split, the Kings of the Northern Kingdom of Israel and the Southern Kingdom of Judah, you will see some righteous kings and some wicked kings. But still God remained with His people and called them to holiness. They failed more than they succeeded, but God still kept his promise to King David. Now God keeps His promise to the Church that "the gates of hell shall not prevail against it." (Matthew 16:18)

Here's a story I heard once on Catholic radio (I believe it was by Peter Kreeft) that makes my point in a humorous way:

---

"In the Middle Ages there was a prominent Jewish merchant that lived in the city of Paris. One day he approached the archbishop and told him that he desired to convert to Catholicism. The bishop was overjoyed that his old acquaintance had embraced Jesus and offered to baptize him on the spot.

The merchant agreed to be baptized, but on one condition, that he first travel to Rome and see the seat of power of this church that he was about to join. Now the bishop was upset, surely he would arrive in Rome and see the decadent and hedonistic nature of the city and even the papacy of pope Alexander VI, a pope known for his less than papal behavior and corruption, so he tried to talk him out of going but the merchant wouldn't be dissuaded.

Six months went by and the merchant finally returned, and as he said he asked to be baptized. The bishop was shocked and said, "You went to Rome and did business with the Vatican and you still want to become Catholic?!?"

The merchant responded, "Look, I'm a practical businessman, and one thing I know is this; any organization so poorly ran and as corrupt as this wouldn't have lasted fifteen days after the resurrection, let alone 1500 years. It's a miracle and God must be with you, I want in!"

---

The point he was making was that despite the incompetence, and sinful men, that sometimes found themselves in the seats of power, it was always really God in control, and since He is all holy, so is His Church.

Our Personal Call to Holiness

Though the Church is Holy despite the men and women

that make it up, it doesn't lessen our own call to holiness. Saint Peter quoted what God said to the people of Israel (Lev 20:26) in his first epistle when he said,

"As obedient children, do not be conformed to the passions of your former ignorance, but as he who called you is holy, be holy yourselves in all your conduct; since it is written, " You shall be holy, for I am holy."

— (1 PETER 1:14-16)

It is impossible to be holy, in and of ourselves, because we are all sinners and apart from God and His holiness we cannot be counted as righteous (Romans 3:10). But God gives us His graces, especially in frequent reception of the sacraments, and through this Grace we can be partakers of the Divine Life and co-heirs to the eternal life of God.

"His divine power has granted to us all things that pertain to life and godliness, through the knowledge of him who called us to his own glory and excellence, by which he has granted to us his precious and very great promises, that through these you may escape from the corruption that is in the world because of passion, and become partakers of the divine nature."

— (2 PETER 1:3-4)

---

Belief in The Church

If you look at the structure of the Nicene Creed, it professes faith in the Father, The Son, the Incarnation, Christ's passion, the Holy Spirit, and the Four Marks of The Church.

It may seem odd, at first glance that we profess our belief in the three Persons of the Holy Trinity, and an institution in the same creed. But I believe it is the integral holiness of the Church, and the assistance that this holiness provides to us in attaining our personal call to holiness, that the Four Marks of the Church are professed during the creed.

It is the visible Church that Christ founded; one, holy, catholic, and apostolic that helps His body walk the path that leads to the narrow gate.

CATHOLIC

(See CCC 830-835)

Catholic vs catholic

One of the things that slip by most people is the fact that the word "catholic" in the creed is using a lower-case C. This is because when we say that we believe the church is catholic, we aren't pledging allegiance to our organizational church. After all, when the creed was written at the end of the 4th century, there was only one Church so there would've been no reason to include a pledge of allegiance to a particular church.

The word "catholic," means universal, and predates the Council of Nicaea by a couple centuries when it was used as an adjective to describe the True Church by Saint Ignatius of Antioch. This universality is what we affirm in the Nicene Creed, it is saying that the Church is for all peoples and in all places. So "catholic" with a small c, is an adjective to describe the church and not a name.

It's not a religious pledge of allegiance

When I was a child in parochial school, we'd go to Mass and I'd recite the Nicene Creed with all the rest of the kids, but I'd omit the word "catholic" thinking it some kind of Papist indoctrination. I was a good little Presbyterian and I wouldn't be tricked into pledging alle-

THE BEAUTY OF THE MASS

giance to the Pope that easily. Oh, how wrong I was. Not only was I wrong about the meaning of that particular part of the creed, but also that I would in fact pledge allegiance to the Catholic Church at an Easter vigil in 2016.

## Roots of a Church called Catholic

The one Church founded by Christ has been known as "The Catholic Church" at least as far back as AD107 when it was called such by St Ignatius of Antioch in his letter to the Smyrneans, but the title was mentioned in passing, as if his reader would already be familiar with it so it's safe to assume it goes back even further.

St Irenaeus also called the church Catholic, in his work *Against Heresy.* In both these instances, "catholic" was used to describe the church and not to name the church. Remember that up until the great schism of east and west in 1054, there was only "The Church" and heretics. The concept of denominations was still 1000 years away, and it was still 700 years until there was a split of eastern and western Christians.

All baptized Christians (some in an imperfect manor) are part of this one universal church, founded by Christ, made holy through Him as its head and built on the witness and testimony of His apostles.

"For in Christ Jesus you are all sons of God, through faith. For as many of you as were baptized into Christ have put on Christ. There is neither Jew nor Greek, there is neither slave nor free, there is neither male nor female; for you are all one in Christ Jesus."

— (GALATIANS 3:26-28)

"The Church knows that she is joined in many ways to the baptized who are honored by the name of Christian, but do not profess the Catholic faith in its entirety or have not preserved unity or communion under the successor of Peter."Those "who believe in Christ and have been properly baptized are put in a certain, although imperfect, communion with the Catholic Church."With the Orthodox Churches, this communion is so profound "that it lacks little to attain the fullness that would permit a common celebration of the Lord's Eucharist."

— (CCC 838)

THE BEAUTY OF THE MASS

Universality is the call of the Great Commission

The Church is universal in its calling to reach all peoples. At the end of Christ's mission here on earth, He left the apostles with what is now called The Great Commission.

> "Go therefore and make disciples of all nations, baptizing them in the name of the Father and of the Son and of the Holy Spirit, teaching them to observe all that I have commanded you; and behold, I am with you always, to the close of the age."
>
> — (MATTHEW 28:19-20)

The prevailing thought of the Jewish people at the time of Christ, was that the messiah would establish an earthly kingdom of Jews, for Jews, and by Jews, but Jesus told his disciples that He came for the whole world (John 3:16).

The Jewish people were the vehicle that brought the messiah into the world, but the call to salvation isn't limited to just them. Jesus makes this clear to the woman at the well in John 4, He tells her that salvation is from the Jews, but a time is coming that men (and women) will worship God, not based on where they live or their ethnicity, but they will worship Him in spirit and in truth.

It is a universal call to salvation, and you will find this being lived out on the Church today. In every corner of the globe you will find people worship God in spirit and in truth, in communion with the successor of St. Peter, and in the One Church that Christ built (Matthew 16:18)

This universal call to salvation is also evidenced in Acts chapter 2 when the Apostles spoke to all present in their own language, and the Saint Peter told them this offer of salvation was for all.

---

"For the promise is to you and to your children and to all that are far off, every one whom the Lord our God calls to him."

— (ACTS 2:39)

---

"That are far off" in Greek is *"tois eis markan"* and doesn't mean those far off in time, it means at a great distance. *Markan* literally translates as "great distance." This marken, or those at a great distance, are the people at every corner of the Globe.

Variety in The Church

When most people think of the Catholic Church, they think of the Roman Catholic Church, but this is somewhat of a misnomer. The Roman Rite of the Catholic Church is just one of the many rites in the Catholic Church.

The majority of the world's Catholics are members of the Latin Church, and the Roman rite in particular, but there are 23 particular churches that are just as Catholic as Latin Catholics. These churches are known as Eastern Catholic Churches, not to be confused with Eastern Orthodox. Eastern Catholics are in union with the Pope and are in communion with the magisterium on all matters of faith and morals, they just have different liturgies, theology, and customs in their Churches.

Pope Saint John Paul II, in his encyclical Ut Unum Sint, called the eastern and western churches "the two lungs of the church." The importance of the eastern Catholic Churches shouldn't be lost on Roman Catholics; it is the evidence for all to see that this Church, that we rightly call catholic, is truly the universal church that Christ intended it to be.

APOSTOLIC

(See CCC 857-866)

What does Apostolic mean?

This might be the most misunderstood of the four previous marks. What does it mean to say that the Church is Apostolic? As we see from the *Catechism* (CCC 857), Apostolic means "of the Apostles" and is used in three senses by the Church.

1. The Church was founded on the Apostles

Jesus had many disciples (disciples coming from the Greek word for pupil or student), He had at least 70 at one point (Luke 10:1), but He only had 12 Apostles.

Twelve was a very important number here too, it wasn't by accident that Jesus chose 12 men. There were 12 sons of Jacob (Genesis 49) who became the 12 tribes of Israel. There were also 12 judges of Israel (Book of Judges), before the people begged God for a king. Then there are the 12 gates of the New Jerusalem, and then also the 12 foundation stones of the city on which are written the names of the 12 Apostles.

---

"It had a great, high wall, with twelve gates, and at the gates twelve angels, and on the gates the names of the twelve tribes of the sons of Israel were inscribed; on the east three gates, on the north three gates, on the south three gates, and on the west three gates. And the wall of the city had twelve foundations, and on them the twelve names of the twelve apostles of the Lamb."

— (REVELATION 21:12-14)

Saint Paul wrote that the Church is "built upon the foundation of the apostles and prophets," and noted that Jesus is Himself "the cornerstone" of this Church. (Ephesians 2:20)

How pivotal was/are the Apostles to the kingdom of heaven that the heavenly Jerusalem is built upon them?

So, what's the difference between the two? A disciple is a student, but an Apostle means "one who is sent." The Apostles were the ones that became Christ's inner circle, and the ones He sent out at the Great Commission.

There were only 12 of these Apostles, 11 at the Great Commission because of the suicide of Judas. Jesus tells the 11 that gathered there,

"Go therefore and make disciples of all nations,

baptizing them in the name of the Father and of the Son and of the Holy Spirit, teaching them to observe all that I have commanded you; and behold, I am with you always, to the close of the age."

— (MATTHEW 28:19-20)

---

This commissioning has three elements:

1. They were to go to all nations, fulfilling the universal call to salvation, and fulfilling the promise made to Abraham (Genesis 22:18) that all nations would be blessed through him. (All the Apostles were Jews, and so descendants of Abraham)

2. They were to baptize those that they converted. Baptism being the sacrament that opens the door to the graces of God, and the divine life. (1 Peter 3:21)

3. They were to teach "all that I have commanded you." This is the magisterial authority of the bishops to teach the Church in matters of faith and morals. This teaching authority is infallible when meeting in an ecumenical council or when

the Bishop of Rome (The Pope) teaches ex cathedra.

The power and authority invested in the Apostles

In Matthew 18:18 Jesus gave the Apostles the power and authority of binding and loosing of sins, this authority was reinforced by the Risen Jesus in the Gospel of John (John 20:21-23), when He reaffirmed their authority over sin.

The Apostles were invested with powers that were not given to the rest of Jesus' disciples, another one of these powers was the ability to choose their successors. (That is the third sense used in CCC 857)

One of the most important elements of the Apostles' authority was their teaching authority. This teaching authority is called the magisterium of the Church (coming from the Latin word for teacher "magister"), this teaching authority is passed on in the form of Apostolic Tradition. And that brings us to the second sense of the word Apostolic.

2. The teaching authority of the Apostles

The second sense of the word Apostolic, used in CCC 857, is the teaching authority of the Church. This authority, also called the magisterium, was exercised through the Apostles, and is exercised today through the bishops of the Church.

This "deposit of faith," as the catechism calls it, is also know as Apostolic Tradition. This Tradition is different from cultural or family traditions, in that it was handed down to the Church by Christ and given to the Apostles, who then passed it along to the churches that they established.

What came first, the Bible or the Church?

What you have to understand is that Christianity is not a "religion of the book," the Church didn't come from the Bible; the Bible came from the Church. The vast majority of the New Testament is made up of letters to the various churches, by their very existence this proves that the churches were already up and running before the New Testament was written.

Jesus didn't write anything, except for what he scribbled in the sand (John 8:6), and we don't even know what it said. He also didn't instruct His followers to write anything, He told them to "instruct" and "teach," but never to write (except for in the vision given to Saint John on the isle of Patmos that is recorded throughout the book of Revelation).

Whenever one of the writers of the New Testament appeals to "the Scriptures," he is referencing the Hebrew

Bible (or what we'd now call the Old Testament). The Bereans "searched the scriptures" (Acts 17:11) to see if the message of the Gospel lined up with the Word of God. Considering this was in the first few decades of the Church age, they weren't searching through the Pauline epistles.

The Church predates the Bible and is called the "pillar and bulwark of truth," by the Bible itself (1 Timothy 3:15). The Bible is the inspired Word of God, but divorced from the magisterium and Apostolic Tradition, it can be twisted to mean whatever the reader wants. This twisting of scriptures is evident in the thousands of Protestant denominations that all think the Bible backs up their particular set of doctrines and beliefs. They can't all be right.

The Traditions of Saint Paul

Saint Paul told the Corinthians to maintain the traditions he had taught them;

---

"I commend you because you remember me in everything and maintain the traditions even as I have delivered them to you."

— (1 CORINTHIANS 11:2)

---

Later he told the Thessalonians about the importance of Tradition; "So then, brethren, stand firm and hold to the traditions which you were taught by us, either by word of mouth or by letter." (2 Thessalonians 2:15) and "Now we command you, brethren, in the name of our Lord Jesus Christ, that you keep away from any brother who is walking in idleness and not in accord with the tradition that you received from us." (2 Thessalonians 3:6)

Why was adhering to Tradition so important to Saint Paul? These letters were written 10-15 years before even the first Gospel was written (Gospel of Mark was possibly written in the late AD60s). He was passing on the teachings of Christ in oral form, and then writing letters back to these churches to remind them of what he instructed.

Importance of Apostolic Tradition

Apostolic Tradition was extremely important to the early Church, and still is today. In the early centuries of Christianity there seemed to be a heresy popping up every year, and the safeguarding of the teaching of the Apostles, through the successions of the bishops, is what kept the Church on the right path.

Remember that the local churches may have had copies of an epistle, or maybe a Gospel or two, but most churches didn't have a compiled canon of all 72 books that make up the Bible until at least the late 4th century.

When confronting these heresies, Saint Irenaeus wrote *Against Heresies* that leaned heavily upon apostolic tradition:

"In this order, and by this succession, the ecclesiastical tradition from the apostles, and the preaching of the truth, have come down to us. And this is most abundant proof that there is one and the same vivifying faith, which has been preserved in the Church from the Apostles until now and handed in truth."

— (*AGAINST HERESIES,* BOOK III, CHAPTER 3, P. III)

Saint Irenaeus, when trying to convince a friend that had fallen into Gnosticism, who claimed to have "secret knowledge" that the gnostics taught was from Christ, that if it really was His teachings, then surely He would've passed it on to his Apostles who would've passed it on to their successors. Since Saint Irenaeus, and this friend, both were taught by Saint Polycarp, he appealed to the teachings of Polycarp (who had himself been made bishop of

Smyrna by Saint John the Apostle). Saying that these heresies weren't taught by Polycarp, who was taught by John,
who was taught by Jesus. It becomes like a modern chain
of evidence, in that you know each step of the chain and
who taught whom. It is by preserving this chain of teachings that we can know the authenticity of the teachings.

This brings us to the last sense of the word Apostolic.

3. Apostolic Succession; from St Peter to Pope Francis

Apostolic Succesion is the way in which the Apostles
handed on their authority to their chosen successors, and
they did the same, and so on until the present day.

The first instance that we see, of Apostolic Succesion, is
in the Book of Acts when the Apostles gather to select the
successor of Judas. Saint Peter stood up, quoting the
psalms, he called for the remaining 11 to select a man to
take the "office" once held by Judas,

---

"For it is written in the book of Psalms, 'Let his
habitation become desolate, and let there be no
one to live in it'; and 'His office let another take.'
And they put forward two, Joseph called
Barsab'bas, who was surnamed Justus, and
Matthi'as. And they prayed and said, "Lord, you

know the hearts of all men, show which one of these two you have chosen to take the place in this ministry and apostleship from which Judas turned aside, to go to his own place." And they cast lots for them, and the lot fell on Matthi'as; and he was enrolled with the eleven apostles."

— (ACTS 1:20,23-26)

---

Saint Peter makes clear that there was a difference between Apostles and disciples. There were 120 followers of Christ in that upper room, and there was at least two who had followed Him since the baptism at the Jordan (John 1:29-34), but even these two were not considered Apostles. Then they prayed and selected Mathias as the successor of Judas.

Setting up churches

Wherever the Apostles went they set up churches and taught the people all that Christ had commanded them to observe. When they'd move on to the next town, they'd set up an overseer, or bishop, to be the shepherd of that local church.

Saint Paul personally appointed Titus as the bishop of Crete and Timothy as bishop of Ephesus, the ordination of Timothy is even recalled by Saint Paul in his letters to Timothy,

---

"Do not neglect the gift you have, which was given you by prophetic utterance when the elders laid their hands upon you." (1 Timothy 4:14) & "For this reason I remind you to rekindle the gift of God that is within you through the laying on of my hands"

— (2 TIMOTHY 1:6)

---

Pope Saint Clement I, in his letter to The Corinthians, reminded them of the importance of the episcopal office, and the Apostolic succession that filled that office with valid bishops, who were to lead and guide the flock on behalf of the Good Shepherd who established them in the first place,

---

"Christ therefore was sent forth by God, and the apostles by Christ. Both these appointments, then, were made in an orderly way, according to the will of God. Having therefore received their orders, and being fully assured by the resurrection of our

Lord Jesus Christ, and established in the word of God, with full assurance of the Holy Ghost, they went forth proclaiming that the kingdom of God was at hand. And thus preaching through countries and cities, they appointed the first fruits [of their labours], having first proved them by the Spirit, to be bishops and deacons of those who should afterwards believe. Nor was this any new thing, since indeed many ages before it was written concerning bishops and deacons. For thus says the Scripture in a certain place, I will appoint their bishops in righteousness, and their deacons in faith."

— (*LETTER TO THE CORINTHIANS,*

CHAPTER 42)

And he goes on to say how the Apostles laid out how to select new bishops after they died, so that the Churches would always have pastors and shepherds over them,

"Our apostles also knew, through our Lord Jesus Christ, that there would be strife on account of the office of the episcopate. For this reason, therefore, inasmuch as they had obtained a perfect foreknowledge of this, they appointed those [ministers] already mentioned, and afterwards gave instructions, that when these should fall asleep, other approved men should succeed them in their ministry."

— (*LETTER TO THE CORINTHIANS,*
CHAPTER 44)

---

Fighting Heresy

Just like Irenaeus appealed to Apostolic Succession to prove a Church teaching, later theologians would do the same throughout the centuries. The fact that some modern theologians are teaching doctrines that would've been foreign to the Apostles is enough to disregard them and stick to the Deposit of Faith. This appealing to the early Church is one of the things that most firmly set me on my path towards Catholicism, because when you read the early Church Fathers you can only come away with one conclusion; they were all Catholic.

Tertullian knew the value of Apostolic Succession in preserving the true faith, and he wrote that the heretics of his day were unable to prove their episcopal pedigree, unlike the validly ordained bishops of his day,

---

"Let them produce the original records of their churches; let them unfold the roll of their bishops, running down in due succession from the beginning in such a manner that [that first bishop of theirs ] bishop shall be able to show for his ordainer and predecessor some one of the apostles or of apostolic men, — a man, moreover, who continued steadfast with the apostles. For this is the manner in which the apostolic churches transmit their registers: as the church of Smyrna, which records that Polycarp was placed therein by John; as also the church of Rome, which makes Clement to have been ordained in like manner by Peter. In exactly the same way the other churches likewise exhibit (their several worthies), whom, as having been appointed to their episcopal places by apostles, they regard as transmitters of the apostolic seed. Let the heretics contrive something of the same kind."

— (*THE PRESCRIPTION AGAINST HERETICS,* CHAPTER 32)

---

This still happens today

Even to this day, Apostolic Succession is still with us.

Every bishop, in the Church today, can trace his episcopal lineage back at least 400-500 years, although the unbroken line of bishops goes back all the way to the Apostles themselves (they were bad at record keeping in the Middle Ages).

It's through this unbroken line, stretching back almost 2000 years, that gives us extra assurance in the deposit of faith that was handed down from one bishop to another. Just ponder that for a moment; your bishop is descended from the very Apostles themselves and has the same teaching and disciplinary authority they did by virtue of their Apostlic Succession.

(Adapted from a series of posts on my website, NowThatImCatholic.com )

# BIBLIOGRAPHY

Catholic Church. *"Catechism of the Catholic Church."* 2nd ed. Vatican: Libreria Editrice Vaticana, 2012.

Catholic Church. *"General Instruction of the Roman Missal."* Washington, DC: United States Conference of Catholic Bishops, 2010 www.usccb.org/prayer-and-worship/the-mass/general-instruction-of-the-roman-missal/index.cfm

Catholic Church. *"The Roman Missal"*. Translated by The International Commission on English in the Liturgy. 3rd ed. Washington D.C.: United States Catholic Conference of Bishops. 2011.

Benedict XVI. *"Jesus of Nazareth"*. United States. Ignatius Press, 2011.

Benedict XVI. *"Sacramentum Caritatis"* Vatican, Libreria Editrice Vaticana, 2007

http://w2.vatican.va/content/benedict-xvi/en/apost_exhortations/documents/hf_ben-xvi_exh_20070222_sacramentum-caritatis.html

Paul VI. *"Sacrosanctum Concilium."* Vatican, Libreria Editrice Vaticana, 1963 www.vatican.va/archive/hist_-councils/ii_vatican_council/documents/vat-ii_const_19631204_sacrosanctum-concilium_en.html.

Paul VI. *"Dei Verbum."* Vatican, Libreria Editrice Vaticana, 1965

www.vatican.va/archive/hist_councils/ii_vatican_council/documents/vat-ii_const_19651118_dei-verbum_en.html

Pius XII. *"Mediator Dei."* Vatican, Libreria Editrice Vaticana, 1947

*http://w2.vatican.va/content/pius-xii/en/encyclicals/documents/hf_p-xii_enc_20111947_mediator-dei.html*

Pius XI. *"Quas Primas."* Vatican, Libreria Editrice Vaticana, 1925

http://w2.vatican.va/content/pius-xi/en/encyclicals/documents/hf_p-xi_enc_11121925_quas-primas.html

John Paul II. *"Ut Unum Sint."* Vatican, Libreria Editrice Vaticana, 1995

http://w2.vatican.va/content/john-paul-ii/en/encyclicals/documents/hf_jp-ii_enc_25051995_ut-unum-sint.html

*The Summa Theologiæ of St. Thomas Aquinas*

Second and Revised Edition, 1920

Literally translated by Fathers of the English Dominican Province

Online Edition Copyright © 2017 by Kevin Knight

Irenaeus. *"Against Heresies"* Translated by Alexander Roberts and William Rambaut. From Ante-Nicene Fathers, Vol. 1. Edited by Alexander Roberts, James Donaldson, and A. Cleveland Coxe. (Buffalo, NY: Christian Literature Publishing Co., 1885.) Revised and edited for New Advent by Kevin Knight. <http://www.newadvent.org/fathers/0103303.htm>.

Tertullian. *"The Prescription Against Heretics"* Translated by Peter Holmes. From Ante-Nicene Fathers, Vol. 3. Edited by Alexander Roberts, James Donaldson, and A. Cleveland Coxe. (Buffalo, NY: Christian Literature Publishing Co., 1885.) Revised and edited for New Advent by Kevin Knight. <http://www.newadvent.org/fathers/0311.htm>.

Clement of Rome. *"Letter to The Corinthians"* Translated by John Keith. From Ante-Nicene Fathers, Vol. 9. Edited by Allan Menzies. (Buffalo, NY: Christian Literature Publishing Co., 1896.) Revised and edited for New Advent by Kevin Knight. <http://www.newadvent.org/fathers/1010.htm>.

Justin Martyr. *"First Apology"* Translated by Marcus Dods and George Reith. From Ante-Nicene Fathers, Vol. 1. Edited by Alexander Roberts, James Donaldson, and A. Cleveland Coxe. (Buffalo, NY: Christian Literature Publishing Co., 1885.) Revised and edited for New Advent by Kevin Knight. <http://www.newadvent.org/fathers/0126.htm>.

Cyprian of Carthage. *"Treatise 4."* Translated by Robert Ernest Wallis. From Ante-Nicene Fathers, Vol. 5. Edited by Alexander Roberts, James Donaldson, and A. Cleveland Coxe. (Buffalo, NY: Christian Literature Publishing Co., 1886.) Revised and edited for New Advent by Kevin Knight. <http://www.newadvent.org/fathers/050704.htm>.

*"Vayikra Rabbah."* Sefaria.org. (2018). [online] Available at: https://www.sefaria.org/Vayikra_Rabbah?lang=bi [

18905528R00116

Made in the USA
Middletown, DE
02 December 2018